Articles,
Articles,
Articles!

Articles,
Articles,
Articles!

Linda Gilden

Bold Vision Books
PO Box 2011
Friendswood, Texas 77549

Copyright © Linda Gilden 2018

ISBN 978194670818-2
Library of Congress Control Number: 2018934585

Cover Design by Maddie Scott

Published in the United States of America.

Published by Bold Vision Books,
PO Box 2011, Friendswood, Texas 77549

Dedication

To the One who loved me
enough to give me the Message
that can change the world.

Table of Contents

Acknowledgments

A writer's job is made so much easier with a strong support system while he or she writes. I have always had that and am so thankful.

My family keeps up with my progress, cheers me on, wears clothes more than once, and eats out more times than you can count without complaining. For all the compromises and sacrifices you had to make during the writing of this book, I love you.

My friends who have faithfully asked, "How's it going?" They let me know what I do matters and they care.

A special thanks to Larry Leech, Lori Hatcher, and Candy Arrington who helped me make the book even better with their suggestions and editorial expertise. And to all the experts who contributed thoughts for the book. A good team is essential for a successful book.

To the Bold Vision Books team, thank you for encouraging me to share my love of article writing. You are the best! I appreciate the opportunity to take others by the hand and lead them to their next steps in article writing. You do your work with excellence, honor God in all you do, and share in the blessing of every reader who holds a BVB book in his or her hands.

Introduction

Early in my college career, I realized the power of words and the impact they have on others. I had written an article I was sure was *Reader's Digest* quality. On my returned paper my teacher wrote, "You have nice handwriting!" Positive words, but for me, a negative message that discouraged me for years to come. My desire to write remained strong.

After many years of volunteer writing for my church and other organizations, my husband said, "I think you ought to try to publish some of your writing in magazines."

"But what about Mrs. Grant. You know what she thought about my writing in college."

"Forget about her," he said. "I know you can do it."

I began to search for information, hoping to find someone or some book that could tell me what I needed to know to submit material to magazines.

When I first started writing, my children were small and still required a lot of hands-on attention. So, my writing sessions were short, very short or nonexistent. Much of what I wrote took place in my head until naptime, then I wrote furiously hoping the children were exhausted and would sleep a long time.

Articles seemed the best option. They didn't require a lot of words, and I could complete one in a short amount of time, especially since I had been doing the mental prewriting. There were so many subject possibilities, and I wanted to learn all the specifics of writing articles. I read everything I could on the subject, which at the time was very little, and I talked to a few published writers. Writing was something I could do at home in between loads of laundry and naps, and it seemed like a good fit.

About the time I became interested in writing, my neighbor and I had a conversation. She, too, had dreams of becoming a writer. She was an English teacher but had no idea where the road to publication started.

One day she walked across the street to my house. "My dad is sending me to a writers conference next month. He thinks you should be my roommate."

"What's a writers conference?" I asked.

"I'm not sure, but it sounds interesting. I think they teach you how to write and there will be editors there wanting to buy your stuff. I thought I might go see what it's like."

My friend and I attended that writers conference and soaked up every bit of knowledge we could. We met "real" writers, editors, and publishers. We learned writers are an essential part of the publishing team.

That conference was life-changing. My first piece was published in a church denominational magazine quickly followed by a devotional series. I was hooked and couldn't imagine ever wanting to write anything other than articles. Ideas were all around me. Article writing was fun and suited my life schedule. I have never lost my love for articles even though I have also written and ghostwritten several dozen books.

Writing articles helped me learn to write tightly, how to say what I wanted to say in as few words as possible, and how to look for a good story and share it with others. Having deadlines and keeping them creates discipline and perseverance. Experiencing the completion of an article and seeing it in print, gave me a taste of success and the excitement of finishing a task.

When my first opportunity came to teach at a writers conference, I felt a little overwhelmed but realized God was opening doors I needed to obediently walk through. Teaching the things that were so exciting to me, my shyness evaporated, and I was focused and energetic. Now I could help not just those in my community but also new writers all over the country.

Articles can change lives. Articles can instruct, inform, and inspire. Articles can open an entirely new world to readers. I love being part of all that.

Whether you have to write during children's naptime, during your lunch break at work, or even if you have all day long to write, the exciting world of magazine writing is open to you as well.

In *Chariots of Fire*, Eric Liddell addressed his sister's concerns about the Olympics interfering with his missionary career in China with this statement, "When I run, I feel God's pleasure." Liddell understood the importance of fulfilling the purpose God had planned for him rather than being successful in the eyes of others.

Looking back on my college days, I remember the power of words. Whether I am writing or teaching someone else how to write, I want my words to point others to the purpose God intends for them.

I am not a runner, but when I write and invest in the lives of other writers, I feel God's pleasure.

Chapter 1
Why Write Articles?

Many authors set their sights on writing books. They see articles as small fish in the publishing sea and not worth the trouble. But writing articles is a great way to start your writing career as you learn how to navigate the publishing industry. Article writing provides many benefits.

Articles are a great way to hone your craft. Writing articles helps you learn to meet deadlines, write within a certain word count, and to write tightly. What is writing tightly? Writing tightly means every word you include in your article must have a purpose. Eliminate all fluff and purge any "rabbit trails." When you have a small word count, you realize how important each word is. As you write just a few pages, you learn how to craft a compelling beginning and ending. Many readers only give you a few seconds to decide if they'll read your work or not.

> Writing tightly means every word you include in your article must have a purpose.

Meeting deadlines is an important part of writing for publication. That deadline is the date your article is due. As writers, it is much better to turn in an assignment early rather than wait until the last minute on the day the article is due. Obviously, you won't literally die if you don't turn an article in on time. But the editor will likely remember you missed a deadline when he or she is deciding who to assign an article to in the future. You want to avoid being on the editor's late list. If, as you work, you find you are not going to make it, contact the editor, explain your good reason for missing the deadline and ask for an extension. Be realistic about how much more time you need and don't miss the new deadline.

Learning to stay within the allotted word count is also a good exercise for new writers, who tend to use too many words when just starting out. Most writers can cut their beginning articles by one third to one half and still not change the meaning of their article.

EXPERT WORD

On tight writing. Forget tight writing and let your draft flow. Then practice tight editing. As Strunk & White advise in *The Elements of Style*, retain only those words that earn their keep. No freeloaders.

In the process you'll replace adverb and adjective phrases with vigorous verbs and evocative nouns. You'll zap empty expressions, such as "for the purpose of" and "in order to." You'll shrink redundant constructions, such as "she nodded her head in agreement." You'll replace pretentious terms and derail long strings of prepositional phrases.

You'll see two benefits. No longer will you struggle to meet tight word counts. And with no excess words clogging your prose, your writing will sing. Fewer words, better words. Everyone wins.

Andy Scheer,
Andy Scheer Editorial Services, www.Andyscheer.com

Articles help build your platform. Your platform is that area in which you are looked upon as an expert. Your name will be associated with the areas of interest you write about, and your name becomes your brand. As a writer, you will hear over and over

> Your platform is that area in which you are looked upon as an expert.

again that you must have a platform. There are many ways to build one, but one of the best ways is to write articles for many different publications. Your name begins to be associated with subjects you write about and invitations to speak will come to you. Building a platform is a lot of work, but in the long run it results in name recognition and increased sales of your articles.

EXPERT WORD

One way to brand yourself as an expert on a topic or subject area is by writing articles for various outlets. In narrowing your focus, you become the go-to person on a subject. Often writers are resistant to niche writing because they fear getting bored writing on the same subject, but you can specialize in more than one area. Just make sure your topics link together. My writing focuses on tough topics: caregiving, aging parents, health, relationships, grief, moving beyond loss, and suicide, and they all overlap in some way.

When you determine your niches, think broadly about possible publishing outlets. You'll be surprised how you can re-slant your topics and expand to related ideas fitting different types of publications. In the process of writing focused articles, you establish your brand.

Candy Arrington, author of *When Your Aging Parent Needs Care: Practical Help for This Season of Life* (www.candyarrington.com)

Articles reach more people than books. Most magazine articles are passed around three to seven times. If you write for a magazine having thousands of readers, your article could reach thousands perhaps millions of readers. Very few books have that reach. Writing articles is a way to extend your influence and wisdom to the world.

Because of the range of articles, they're a great marketing tool for your books. You can list your book in your current bio that goes along with your article thereby reaching all that market's readership with mention of your book.

Speakers need to have a way to extend the reach of their messages. An article is a way to take your message and share it with the world. Speakers have done a lot of research for their speeches, research that can be turned into articles easily. An article not only spreads the word and increases your influence, it can generate a little extra income in the meantime.

Because it doesn't take as long to write an article as it does a book, you can sell articles more quickly and thereby get paid more promptly for what you write. For example, a book can take months if not years to complete. Many writers can write a 1000-word article in a day or two. Doing so on a regular basis brings in tremendous income if you are writing for well-paying publications.

You'll expand your horizons and extend the scope of what you know.

Articles change lives. Your how-to articles help your readers grow because they're learning something new. Your informational, profile, and other articles impart new knowledge to your readers. Your inspirational articles help readers understand themselves better and turn their lives in a positive direction.

AUTHOR NOTE

I have been told by more than one person my articles relating to my book, *Love Notes on His Pillow*, may have saved their marriages. To know you have had such an impact on multiple lives is rewarding and makes all the late-night races to deadlines worth it.

Chapter 2
Getting Started

Often one of the greatest roadblocks to new writers is their perception of themselves as writers. In other words, new writers have trouble thinking of themselves as writers, crossing the line of wannabe writers to "real" writers.

As readers, we look at the authors of the books we read and the articles in magazines and tend to put them on a pedestal. We think they are in a much more learned and lofty position than we could ever be. That is a false notion. If this is your mindset, get rid of it right away. Writers, editors, and publishers are people like you whose jobs happen to be in the publishing industry. They want to do their jobs well so editors are looking for self-confident writers who can craft a well-written story targeted to their audiences.

> Editors are looking for self-confident writers who can craft a well-written story targeted to their audiences.

Begin today to put yourself in the category of professional writer. Wherever you are as you read this, raise your right hand and say aloud, "I am a writer." Do it several times until you become accustomed to the sound of your voice declaring you are a writer. Practice in front of a mirror if you can't choke the words out otherwise. Tell your children, your cat, and your dog. Then you can say with confidence to your friends or anyone else who asks, "I am a writer."

This is the first step in starting your writing career. Self-confidence takes you a long way and help you write with assertiveness. Writers who are less than confident make many mistakes and continue second-guessing themselves until they push the send button on their manuscripts.

There are other ways to build your confidence. Mix with other writers. Join a writers group to help build confidence as you learn alongside your peers. Many towns have writers groups available. Search the internet and market guides to learn if there is one in your town. If not, online groups meet and offer many of the same benefits. These groups meet regularly, offer critique, and conduct instructive classes on many different aspects of writing. Attend a writers conference in your area. Conferences usually have good attendance from those who live nearby and provide multiple opportunities for networking with other writers. These things help you grow your writers community and find encouragement and support.

When you've made the commitment to be a writer, focus on that commitment and get ready to work hard to build your writing career. You *are* a writer!

Your Work Space

New writers often hear more established writers talk about their offices. Having a beautifully decorated office is a dream for many writers. However, your office doesn't have to be out of a decorator magazine. The important thing is you have a dedicated space for your writing. Dedicated means you have someplace where you most likely find your computer and all the research for your work-in-progress. For some writers, it may be the dining room table. For others, it may be a corner of the bedroom, kitchen, or playroom. Finding a space somewhere other than your bedroom is probably best so work is not the first thing you see in the morning and the last thing you see every night.

Whatever space you establish as your writer space should be observed as such. When you are sitting at your "desk," in your "office," the family should know you are not to be disturbed for anything short of blood or fire! They should respect your few minutes to retreat to your writing spot and do their best to help you make the most of your time.

Your family can be of great help in protecting your time. If you are writing, have them answer the phone or the door. It is perfectly acceptable for them to say you are unavailable. You are. You are at work as if you had left the house and gone into town to an office where you would be unavailable until after office hours. Enlist help with the laundry, cooking supper, or cleaning the house. If you ask with an appreciative attitude and maybe a reward or two attached, you may find your family more willing to help with the chores.

Surround yourself with objects that make you feel peaceful and calm. Candles, books, family pictures and a few flowers sometimes bring the personal touch to an otherwise mundane spot.

If you can't find a suitable space to write in your home, find a coffee shop, library, or park where you feel comfortable and inspired. You don't want to get too relaxed because this is not naptime. You need a place where your creative juices can flow with a minimum of distractions.

Hopefully, some day you will have the kind of office you dream of with beautiful bookshelves laden with reference books and shelves and shelves of your books. Just remember the place you write has no effect on the quality of words you put on your paper. Write your best wherever you are.

Your Work Habits

When you have established your office, a place specifically yours for writing, look at your work habits. Are you at a place in your life where you can have office hours or do you need to write after the family has gone to bed at night? Do you have a job that takes you outside your home during the week, so weekends are your primary writing time? Are you a caregiver or young mom whose focus must be on someone else most of the time?

Try writing at different times of the day and see when you feel most productive. Make that your primary writing time so you can get the most accomplished in what time you have. If you can establish some sort of schedule, it helps you and your friends know when you are planning to write and help you keep that time sacred. Turn off the phone and let voicemail take the messages. Don't answer the door unless you are expecting a package or other delivery. Don't push yourself to write when your focus needs to be somewhere else. Make the most of the writing time you have, and the job will get done. Stress is your enemy and can become more of a distraction than a help.

> Make the most of the writing time you have, and the job will get done.

AUTHOR NOTE

My early writing days were also my early parenting days. My children required constant supervision or attention. I wrote all day long in my head. Then when naptime rolled around or the children were in bed for the night, I went to my keyboard and got everything out of my head onto paper. Sometimes I didn't have more than ten or fifteen minutes. I learned how to make the most of even those small snatches. The next day I began the process all over again. Eventually, I finished an article, submitted it, and was ready to start on the next project. Yes, it took me much longer to write an article then than it does today, but I persevered and found my way into the publishing world.

For many years, I operated on the principle if my family needed me, I should put their needs as top priority. Many times, I had to leave the computer to take care of someone's needs— someone to whom it didn't make a lot of difference that my dream was to be a writer! But I believe, and always have, family should come first. If they need me, I want to be there. God has never failed to redeem time I took away from my writing and gave to my family.

Chapter 3
Magazine Articles, E-zines, and Blogs

When you write magazine articles, there are many decisions to think about such as what market to target. Two main divisions in magazine writing are general market publications and religious/inspirational publications.

General market magazines are those that target the universal population and cover many subjects.

Consumer magazines are directed to the public, provide advertising geared toward them, and are written from a wide viewpoint. Some examples of consumer magazines are *People, Family Circle, Time,* and similar publications. People in the industry sometimes call them "glossies" because they are printed on glossy paper. Many of the home decorating, travel magazines, etc. fall into the general market category as do trade magazines. Trade magazines target a specific industry and cover topics of specific interest to that industry, such as hunting, cars, or window washers. Almost every industry has one. Many of these magazines are found

Trade magazines target a specific industry and cover topics of specific interest to that industry, such as hunting, cars, or window washers.

on the newsstands and at bookstores. Some are by subscription only since the specific readership is easier to identify. General market magazines also publish inspirational pieces, but their purpose is to inform the public rather than introduce them to faith. General marketing magazines usually pay higher rates to authors. Writers can have a huge impact on the world writing for these publications.

Christian and inspirational markets, on the other hand, present many opportunities for Christian writers to share their faith and point others to the Gospel. *Guideposts* is one of the best known in this market and offers writers the opportunity to share their personal stories and the stories of others. Breaking into the magazine market is sometimes a little easier in the Christian and inspirational markets, but it is generally a lower paying market and circulation is often smaller than general market magazines.

Writing for print and writing for the web, though similar, are two different processes. Although both involve putting words on the page, the audiences are looking for a different type of information and receive it in a different way.

Print Articles

Most readers of magazine articles have a more leisurely approach to their reading and settle in to discover what the writer has to say on a certain subject. Readers expect to find stories to back up the points as they are made. Graphics such as charts, graphs, and diagrams enhance understanding of the subject. Magazine readers expect to spend several minutes reading a full article.

Writing for print is for a finite audience. You may not know the exact number who read the articles because there are subscriptions, newsstand sales, and readers who have been given the magazine when someone else has finished with it.

When readers pick up a magazine, it's because they have a specific interest in the subject of the magazine. Before opening the magazine, the reader knows what is inside has benefit in some way for him or her. Writers have targeted those readers because they know the demographics of the readership before they begin to write.

Seeing your articles in print is a thrill and a responsibility. The reader looks upon you as the expert, the authority, the king or queen of the subject. Don't disappoint your reader. Make sure you do your job well so when you see your article in print you'll be proud.

EXPERT WORD

One of the best things you can do early on is to learn the types of articles specific magazines publish and then pitch those types with a unique hook. For example, say something like, "I know you publish a number of round up articles about homeschooling. I'm proposing an 800-word round up article from four different perspectives from families who homeschool for non-religious reasons."

You can also offer to write hard-news articles for newspapers, but if you do, learn to use the inverted pyramid structure newspapers prefer. (The inverted pyramid structure is used by journalists to show how to prioritize your information. The most important information is in the widest portion of your pyramid which is upside down. This corresponds to the beginning of your article. In the middle of your pyramid are the details pertaining to the information already stated. The bottom part of the pyramid (the point) contains the least important information, backstory, or details that could be left out. This method is valuable to newspapers because if they need to edit the article because of space constraints, they can begin cutting at the bottom knowing the more important facts are at the top.)

Lee Warren is the author of *Write That Devotional Book* and *Write That Book in 30 Days*. www.leewarren.info.

Web Articles

Readers who come to the web for information are on a hunt. They are looking for a solution to a problem and want to find it fast. They have not come to read endless amounts of what they consider

25

extra verbiage and fluff. Web content must be brief and to the point. Readers want content they can act upon and use immediately.

Web readers aren't there for the pleasure of reading; they are there for the fast-informational result. They want concise writing that yields results. Web readers want writers to get to the point and get to it quickly. They have typed the subject into a search engine and chosen the top few sites seeming to answer their questions. They quickly peruse a site to see if what they are looking for is there. Experts on the subjects say even their method of reading is different starting in the middle of the page rather than the left side.

A keyword is a word connecting your article to a particular subject and is used by search engines to point readers to related web documents.

Writing for the web requires writers to take all these differences into consideration.

Writers must know how to use keywords. A keyword is a word connecting your article to a particular subject and is used by search engines to point readers to related web documents. Using keywords gives your article a broader reach and brings more targeted readers to your article. If you are writing content for major websites, provide some keywords.

Headlines are an important aspect of web writing. Headlines hook with a flair. Good headlines tell the reader what the article is about but incorporate intrigue as well. Think about something you might tweet. Just a few words are allowed so each word must be chosen carefully. Your tweet, just like your headline, will probably only be glanced at, so it needs to be strong. There is not a lot of room to be clever or cute. Web readers love great headlines because they don't have to skim the article to see if it contains the information they are looking for. Being conscious of search engine optimization helps you to create a strong headline with keywords easily found by web surfers.

EXPERT WORD

Keywords ultimately "connect the dots." Each keyword has a specific set of searches performed every month. If your keywords have no searches, they might not bring any traffic. If you target the right words when writing your article, you could draw in hundreds if not thousands of targeted readers interested in your topic.

Jeff Gilden, Charlotte SEO Expert, Search Engine Optimization Company and Internet Marketing Firm in Charlotte NC
www.charlotteseofirm.com

You may wonder if a headline is the same as a title. No, it's not. Your headline directs traffic to your article which will possibly have a different title. A title can tell the reader what the article is about but often the title is catchy and may not contain both subject and verb. The title would also contain keywords so those searching for the subject can find it.

Good headlines tell the reader what the article is about but incorporate intrigue as well.

For example,
```
Headline—"Twins Barely
Survive An Impossible Separation!"
Title—"Formerly Conjoined Twins Sent
to Different Rehab Centers"
```

Images are also important part of web writing. Pictures convey additional information or enhance the words you've written. Web readers are drawn to the images as a means of evaluating whether to read on. So, select your images carefully. Some websites select images for you and others add them when your article is submitted.

In writing for the web, careful attention needs to be given to your first few sentences because the reader decides in a few seconds whether or not to read on. Your promise of pertinent information needs to be filled quickly in your web articles.

EXPERT WORD

The most important considerations when writing for the internet are your headline, images, and first paragraph, which is usually five to six lines. The dance between headlines and first paragraph is this: The headline tells the punch line and makes you want to know the story. The first paragraph satisfies the intrigue and creates another one. That's the difference.

Rhonda Robinson, Managing Editor for
MondayMondayNetwork.com

With the opportunity to link your article to more information, web writers can provide readers with the option of pursuing additional information without encumbering the main information they want to transmit. Readers are free to take the general information or they can follow the trail left by the writer to enhance their learning even more. Linking to other articles is not competing with your article. It is providing extra value to your writing which your readers appreciate.

Many magazines post their print articles on the web which increases the reach of your article. That information will be in your contract.

Some magazines also post additional articles on their websites. Those articles were never in their magazines. Submitting to the print segment of the magazine is different than submitting to the web segment of the magazine. There are different editors for each segment and what they look for is different both in style and content. If you want to write for a magazine that also buys content for their website, study the site just like you would study a print magazine. Magazine and information websites are divided into channels, sometimes also called verticals. These subject areas provide opportunities for writers. Search the site for the name of the editor of the site or channel. This is a different editor than for the print version of the magazine.

Print Articles vs.	Web Articles
You never know exactly who reads your article.	You can know the frequent audience to the website.
Word count is usually longer—could be as much as 2,000 or 3,000 words.	Word count is usually shorter. Longer print articles must be reduced to a few hundred words for the web.
Can use more words to support the point through anecdotes, stories, facts, and charts.	Must use a more journalistic, inverted pyramid approach.
Readers are usually looking for an entertaining and informative read and are willing to stick with you.	Readers typically scan the material, picking out what is most important to them.
Cover lines and newsstands must draw readers to the magazine.	You must use keywords to make sure readers find your work.
You can provide references but not direct links.	Linking to other sites provides your reader more information and increases credibility.
Users are looking for information in a more leisurely fashion.	Users want information quickly.
Reader has already committed when buying the print piece so is already hooked.	Hook must be strong because article is vying for readership with many other outlets.
Generally pay more.	Often pay less (but not always).
Readers read the entire article.	Readers scan to find what they need.
Readers must take the initiative to search for more information.	Links can provide the reader with more information on the subject without adding more research time.
Once written is unchangeable.	Can be rewritten and updated.

Blogs

In the late '90s weblogs came on the scene. These shorter, more personal articles brought a chatty, conversational style of writing to the web. By the end of the decade they received their shortened name, blogs, and became a popular form of communication. Many days the number of blogs posted totals several million. If you would like to check out the number of posts as you are reading, visit worldometers. info/blogs.

In the beginning, blogs permitted writers to share their passion about a certain subject. People read widely and studied the subject and their blogs were just a natural overflow of their excitement about the subject. The more blogs they posted the better known they became in their fields.

As time has passed, the popularity of blogs has grown. Many blog writers often invite guest writers, or guest bloggers, to fill in for them or give them a break. Some bloggers have restructured their blogs to include other writers on a regular basis.

Businesses now often have blogs to encourage the readers and those interested in their products to think through issues related to their businesses. Business blogs are not infomercials. They are informative and educate the reader. If they do a good job, the reader migrates to their products to have the best available products if the business provides quality services.

Many writers now supplement their incomes nicely through writing for business blogs. Business blog sites can pay from nothing up to $1 or so a word for a post of around 500 words.

If you want to get started writing copy for business blogs, look at business websites. A good place to start is with those in your town or state. If you find a business with a nice website but no blog, study the site then contact the business with some suggested blogs and how the blog could be positive for the business. Write a sample blog or two and send them to the business.

Here are a few helpful tips if you are just starting out as a blogger.

- You must blog regularly and on a schedule. Readers don't have time to keep checking your site to see if you happened to have blogged each day. Make a commitment to your readers to blog regularly at least once a week, and they will stick with you.

- Pick an interesting and inviting title for your blog telling your readers what they will receive from the blog. Think of subjects people might search the web for or questions they might like to have answered. Incorporating those words into your title makes it easier for the search engines to find you.

Although blogging may seem a more casual and relaxed form of writing, work hard to make sure your writing you post on your blog is just as good writing as other forms of writing. Posting the blog on the web begins to get your name out there, and you don't want it to be associated with anything other than excellent writing.

Stay focused. You don't have to write on the same subject every time, but whatever you talk about should reflect your brand. Many of the successful blogs target a specific group of readers such as writers, animal enthusiasts, musicians, parents, etc.

Make sure the value is there for your readers no matter what the length of your blog. Some people perceive a blog must be short because it is online writing. Short is good, but if you have more than 500 words to say, don't be afraid to say it.

Use images to enhance your blog and draw readers to it. Just be sure to use images with proper licensing for your needs.

Use your name as the site URL. This helps you build your platform and makes it easier for people to find you.

At the end of your blog post, leave your readers with a challenge or question to keep them thinking about the subject you have written about. If you add a comment section, readers can not only think about their responses but also share them with each other.

Include ways for your readers to share your blog on social media. Create tweets requiring only a click or two for the readers to post.

Provide a way for your readers to subscribe to your blog so they receive an alert in their mailboxes when a new blog is posted. You can use both email signups and RSS (Really Simple Syndication).

When your blog is up and operational, you need to work to bring readers to your site. Social media is a good way to do this. Make a big announcement about your new blog and ask your friends to share as well. Entice readers with a giveaway or promise of exciting new information. Make sure you have used strong keywords in your blog so people easily find you.

RSS is a way of reading blogs through a reader.

Chapter 4
Ideas

Where do you get ideas?

Ideas are all around you. Writers must train themselves to be alert to the world around them, to the current news, and to possible stories within their spheres of influence. Florence Littauer, founder of CLASS, Christian Leaders Authors Speakers Seminars, teaches participants to be "alert to life." "Alert to life" is to be aware of what is happening around you so you can create springboard articles from them. Be aware of the happenings in your life that could be good illustrations for your speaking and writing. Learn how to look at the ordinary and see a practical or spiritual application.

> "Alert to life" is to be aware of what is happening around you so you can create springboard articles from them.

For example, if you drive up to a four-way stop and see a bright red minivan already stopped there. You glance over at the minivan and realize the person in the driver's seat is not really looking to see how many other cars are stopped at the intersection. The driver is smiling and applauding wildly. What could possibly be happening in that minivan to illicit such celebration?

Of course, you don't know. The preteen in the passenger seat could have just handed a stellar report card to his mother. Or maybe the toddler in the backseat had just retrieved his or her pacifier without Mom having to stop the car and assist. Maybe the favorite family song just started playing on the radio and they didn't want to miss a chance to do a little car dancing. No matter what the occasion, there was celebration going on in that minivan.

This short, unexpected scene can be the springboard for a number of articles or talks. The first thing that came to my mind is we all need applause. A great article or talk on encouragement could come from your observation.

Or you might go in another direction. Families need each other. That article could spotlight ways family members could support other family members. You could write an article with more of an adult slant or focus on how children can be supportive of each other and of their parents.

Another direction might be the crossroads of life. When you come to a stop sign what comes to your mind? What about the other folks at the stop sign? How can you possibly know what is going on in their lives?

You see how this "alert to life" thing works. When you observe something as an illustration for a point, there are usually multiple ways you can use it.

EXPERT WORD

Coming up with ideas is never a problem if you're a writer. Your mind should always be running at full speed as you think, *That could be an article . . . and that could be . . . and that could be.* The problem is knowing which ones are *best*. If your idea has been done before with the same focus/angle, chuck it. Move to the next one.

The best ideas come from actively listening to the world around you. Open your ears and your mind will follow.

Ginger Kolbaba, award-winning author and editor,
www.gingerkolbaba.com

Ideas are all around you. Where are the best places to find them?

Home

What better place to find ideas than the place you spend most of your time? If your house is anything like mine, there is something going on all the time.

Walk into the front door of your home and pretend you have never been there before. Look around. Are there any collections? Family pictures? Picture-perfect decorations? Evidence of children? A walker or cane? Everything you see is likely an idea-starter, and if you let your creative mind wander, you will come up with lots of possibilities for articles.

John is having some back problems. A year from now, hopefully he won't be having back problems. In the midst of centering his thoughts on back health, however, what a great time for him to write an article about "How to Keep Your Back Strong," "8 Exercises to Make Bending Easier," "Alternate Treatment for Back Sufferers," etc. A lot of what he talks about is back-problem related. He is doing a lot of research as to how to help himself so the subject is fresh on his mind. Soon he will be on the other side with even more information.

It is back to school time for children. "Love Notes in Lunchboxes," "Making Sure Your Child is Ready," or "Back to School and Sports" are all good possibilities for this time of year.

Margaret and Frank have an annual grandchildren's camp. Article ideas abound that would be helpful to encourage families to do fun activities together. "Cousin's Camp," "8 Fun Meals for 8 Cute Kids," "Games Even Grandparents Can Play" are just a few possible ideas.

Holidays are natural celebration days for families. What are some of the unique ways you have celebrated Labor Day, Thanksgiving, Christmas, Ground Hog Day, or even a lesser known day such as National Left-Handers Day?

Relationships

You want to be careful here not to betray any trusts and make sure you have permission if you write about a specific relationship.

Have you worked through a difficult time with a friend? Writing "7 Ways to Keep Friendships Strong" may give you a voice to help others avoid strained relationships. Have you discovered ways to grow relationships with family members or make holidays easier when you have lots of people together? "Keeping Holidays Jolly" will suggest ways for readers to keep peace during the holidays and help everyone have a great time.

Do you have a friend who has done something special or unusual? Honor them by writing a profile article. These types of articles are the mainstay of magazines so they are always looking for them. Even children's magazines use profiles of children who are making a difference in the world.

AUTHOR NOTE

In another part of our state, there is an annual Kudzu Festival. I heard about it and thought a general article about the festival would be interesting to people in our state. Kudzu was brought over from Japan in the late 1800s as a means of stopping erosion. (Kudzu grows at the rate of about a foot per day and is so prolific in our area new test sites have been created to figure out how to get rid of it!) The festival article went well, but in my research, I learned about other related subjects. I wrote about the kudzu fashion show, kudzu jelly, kudzu basket making, and a few others. One idea about a festival in my area, spawned several different ideas to write about.

News

Current events often cause your mind to get excited about a subject, wonder about something, ask why an event happened, etc. Often you get new ideas for articles from other articles. Read your newspaper with an eye toward the unusual or toward subjects leaving questions unanswered. Listen or watch the news and look for an open door for an article to take the subject a little deeper.

Look for local news stories you can turn into inspirational articles for a national audience. Likewise, what national story can you scale down or make applicable to the people who live near you?

Personal Experience

Everyone has experiences. And if it happened to you, it is your personal experience and a great springboard for article ideas. If you had a flat tire on the interstate with two crying toddlers in the car and it was almost dark and no one else was with you and you were thirty miles from home, what would you do? Topics from the experience might include "6 Ways to Entertain Small Children in the Car," "Emergency—Best Place to Get Help," or you may share a description of the experience and how you discovered a strength you didn't even know you possessed.

Are You an Expert?

When you think of experts you may think of those who have multiple degrees behind their names and are much sought after for interviews and television appearances. Most of us are experts at something. Your every day activities may have become almost habit, but they may not be habits to everyone. Perhaps you have a big family and wash several loads of clothes a day. You are probably an expert on the best way to remove stains, which setting to use on the washing machine (Most have multiple settings and few are used because users don't know what they are really for.), or how to keep your washer from "eating" socks.

If you are an outdoor person and often win "Yard of the Month," others would probably like to know what your yard regimen is. If you grow prized irises or calla lilies, could you share your secret?

Do you know an expert?

If you don't consider yourself an expert at anything (which is likely not true), surely you know an expert. If you want to write an article on "10 Secrets for Buying a Car," you may not know those 10 tips off the top of your head. Chances are you have bought a car or know someone who sells them. Call and ask to interview them.

Prepare a list of questions to help guide the conversation. Your expert may come up with 20 secrets and you would have enough for more than one article.

If you don't know an expert personally, colleges and universities are a good place to look for experts. A phone call explaining what you are looking for can usually result in a scheduled interview with the expert.

Overcoming Obstacles

Many of your best articles come from lessons you have learned. Have you faced a difficult time in your life and discovered a solution to also help others? Did you make a move across the country with four children under the age of 5 and learned a few ways to make it easier for young families who were relocating? Have you lost a loved one and discovered coping techniques to help those who have experienced the same kind of loss? Have you overcome depression and now live a full and happy life focused on your family? How did you get through it?

If you have overcome something, whether it is a physical, emotional, mental, or a spiritual challenge, chances are someone else is dealing with it too and could use some encouraging words from someone who is on the other side of the difficulty.

Faith

Believers need to look no further than their daily devotion and Bible reading time for ideas to encourage and uplift others. Readers need to hear from people who are growing closer to God. Hearing how others have discovered ways to draw near to God helps readers want to do the same. Articles on how to grow in your faith, particularly with a step-by-step process, are well received and can have life changing effects.

School

School-related articles are always popular, especially during the back to school season. Parents are always looking for ways to make the school year easier and less stressful for the family. Also, thinking about school suggests subjects such as "Easy Lunchbox Recipes," "Dress for Success-Helping Your Child Manage His Wardrobe," and "7 Ways to Make the Most of the Carpool Line."

Work

The workplace abounds with ideas for articles to help people find success. You may have found a way to do your job better specific to your company. A company newsletter would be the ideal place. If your company is a national company, there may be a company magazine or national newsletter. If you have discovered how to do something in a general category such as how to file more efficiently, 10 ways to be the best receptionist ever, or the best computer program to manage payroll, it will appeal to business publications of all kinds. Perhaps there have been issues within your company with authority, time management, or personalities/relationships. Your solutions to those issues would help others in the business world who are dealing with similar situations.

Natural Disasters

Hurricanes, floods, fires, blizzards and other natural disasters prompt ideas for articles. How did you survive when the power was out for more than a week? Does your house freeze when snow is over the top of the roof? Were you rescued from your house during a flood? Your personal experience including your feelings would make an excellent article. Look for opportunities to write about these on anniversary dates. Some events warrant an update article even ten or twenty years later. Talk to survivors and find out how the natural disaster impacted their family and work life.

Billboards and public service announcements

Keep your eyes and ears open to see who might be coming to your area. This is a great opportunity to interview someone for a profile article. Often a speaker or celebrity comes to an area for a speaking engagement and has blocks of time with nothing to do. This free time opens the door to schedule an interview and is both good for you and for them.

Contact the event planner or promoting organization, explain you would like to interview their guest and ask if he or she would give you the contact information or put you in contact with someone who could, such as a publicist or manager. The speaker or celebrity is excited about the possibility of getting some unexpected publicity while in the area. If there is time, do a phone interview and pitch an article to your local paper before the event.

AUTHOR NOTE

One of the best tips for an article came from none of the above. My washing machine repairman was fixing my washer. He stuck his head out from behind the washing machine and he said, "Have you ever written a story about a fellow who lives about five miles from here? I fixed his daughter's washing machine yesterday."

"I don't guess I have because I'm not sure who you are talking about. What's his name?"

"Charles. He has written some of the songs a popular gospel group sing. You know who the Gaithers are? They sing Southern Gospel."

My interest level just went up. "Of course, I know the Gaithers. I love their music. You mean they sing his music on TV?"

"Sure do."

"I'd love to talk to him. Can you put me in touch with his daughter?

"I would be glad to. Will call you as soon as I talk to her."

"Thanks."

This was not the most conventional way to line up an interview. But I enjoyed the interview and was happy to be able to place the story in several places. When I knew this little-known celebrity was right in my backyard, I was excited to introduce him to the world.

Brainstorming

One of the best ways to generate and flesh out ideas is to brainstorm with other writers. Your fellow writers are some of your most valuable resources. Brainstorming can happen spontaneously in a very casual and informal setting or as part of a regularly scheduled meeting.

> One of the best ways to generate and flesh out ideas is to brainstorm with other writers.

Brainstorming is a simple process whereby you state your idea then allow time for your colleagues to comment. They may suggest ways to strengthen the article, new slants, multiple article ideas from your research, or give ideas for markets interested in your work.

When you present an idea to a brainstorming group, you state your idea simply. Then you wait for the comments of others. For instance, Rick may bring an article idea called "The Joy of Man's Best Friend." Rick's idea was to write about his dog and the close relationship they had.

As his brainstorming group began talking, Grace said, "That's a great idea and I'm sure it benefits dog owners. Write a personal experience article. Why don't you also write a practical how-to about 'The Care and Feeding of Man's Best Friend?' I'm sure you have had lots of related experiences."

Scott spoke up. "Yes, and you can write about special characteristics of German Shepherds since Hank is a German Shepherd. Maybe you could even market a brochure or pamphlet to the German Shepherd Dog Club of America."

"You know, I recently heard of using dogs for therapy for the elderly," said Marilyn. "What a great article! You could even do a local version and a national one."

"Yes, and while you are doing research, you could gather quotes from families who had benefitted from therapy dogs and create a round-up article. Rick, I think this idea is a great idea," Lucy said.

Rick chuckled. "Actually, I only had one idea. You guys are the best. Now I have lots of different articles from my one idea."

Rick's experience is not unique. When you assemble a group of creative minds in just minutes you can come up with ways you never thought of to use and reuse your research.

If you are not part of a group like this, why not form one. Invite a few like-minded writers to your house and ask them to bring just one idea. It doesn't have to be something they are currently working on. Maybe there is a subject they have had rolling around in their heads for some time and never fleshed it out.

When people experience the profitability, practicality, and yes, even fun, of brainstorming this way, they will be anxious to do it again and again. And the more they do it, not only will they want to brainstorm with friends, but they learn how to do the same thing for themselves when they are alone.

It's easy to see the many possibilities for one article idea if you make a simple chart.

Take a blank piece of paper and make two columns and ten rows. You can add rows as needed. See the chart on the next page as an example.

See how one thought can lead to another? Even thinking of therapeutic dogs and how they can visit nursing homes and the elderly reminds us of another idea totally unrelated to dogs but spring-boarded from the original subject of dogs.

When you make your chart, you will have plenty of work for a while. Since you have determined you will write many articles on one subject, you can keep several files as you do your research—one for each article. As you research, categorize your facts and be diligent about organizing them so you can easily access the information. When your research is complete, you have multiple files from which to write and can pitch a number of articles within a short amount of time.

General Topic	**Dogs**
Specific Idea	The Joy of Man's Best Friend
Another Slant (How-To)	The Care and Feeding of Man's Best Friend
Informational Slant	German Shepherds—A Great Breed
Health Slant	Therapeutic Best Friends
Another Health Slant (Round-Up)	Benefits of Therapy Dogs
Unrelated New Idea	How to Choose a Nursing Home for Your Loved One
Another Slant (possibly women's magazines)	Companion Dogs
Travel Slant	Easy Vacationing with Your Pet (could be limited to dogs or include other pets)
Sports Slant (possibly for a men's or hunting magazine	Tandem Hunting – A Good Hunting Dog is the Best Companion
Family Slant (parenting magazines)	Children and Pets – When is the Best Age to Get a Pet

Clustering

Clustering is similar to brainstorming. First thing you do is to create an inner circle with your main subject. For the chart below, we look at the same general subject of dogs (middle circle) and layer additional circles around the main topic.

You can have as many circles as you want. For this illustration, I chose five circles for the next layer. Notice how the next layer still is on the subject of dogs but becomes a bit more specific.

Radiating from those five circles, are more ideas sparked by each circle. For this chart, we stayed close to the main subject of dogs. However, sometimes when you brainstorm in this manner, by

43

the time you get to the third layer of circles, your mind has taken a totally different direction and you begin to include slightly related but different subjects.

For instance, when we look at the circle near the bottom saying "Therapy Dogs," you may look at the subject of "Dogs for Special Needs" and begin to think of other subjects related to Special Needs instead of Dogs. You may think of dogs that can smell an epileptic seizure twenty minutes before it happens and the thought takes you down the trail of ideas about epilepsy. Or you have observed a dog for autism therapy. Some people with mental anxiety also have therapy dogs which allow them to function calmly in public. All those subjects are great article ideas. In fact, you could start a new chart with the subject of "Therapy Dogs" in your middle circle and go from there.

Using a visual to help you define what topics are viable or not is an easy way to see what topics are gold mines and which ones really can't be developed into much. Concentrate on the areas where you have lots of ideas.

Do you see how this exercise can give your creativity a boost and help you create many article possibilities from one main idea?

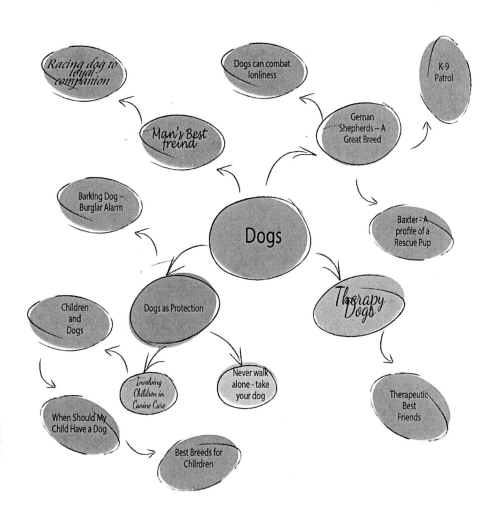

Racing dog to loyal companion

Dogs can combat lonliness

K-9 Patrol

Man's Best freind

Gernan Shepherds -- A Great Breed

Barking Dog -- Burglar Alarm

Dogs

Baxter - A profile of a Rescue Pup

Children and Dogs

Dogs as Protection

Therapy Dogs

Involving Children in Canine Care

Never walk alone - take your dog

Therapeutic Best Friends

When Should My Child Have a Dog

Best Breeds for Chilrdren

AUTHOR NOTE

Brainstorming or clustering with a few friends or a writers group can be both beneficial and fun.

Years ago, I wrote materials for a national sports ministry, and the ministry planning meetings could get exciting. The others who attended the meetings weren't writers, but they were extremely creative individuals. As we talked and planned the written materials for the month, they sometimes got so excited they would jump to their feet to emphasize their idea was better than the rest had presented. I loved the high energy in the room and the focus on helping me do my job better. I had plenty to write about for quite a while!

Chapter 5
Breaking In

New writers often ask the question—How can I break in to the magazine market?

When you have decided you want to write articles for magazines, blogs, and websites you become much more attentive to the content they are using. Many magazines publish weekly. Others publish monthly or bimonthly. All need lots of material.

A good place to start is with magazines you read often. Because you enjoy them and are familiar with the types of articles they publish in each issue, you will find it easier to write to fit the magazine's style. Knowing what subjects the magazine covers and the slants they use make writing for magazines you like easier to submit to.

Several general categories of magazines exist, all with plenteous opportunities for writing articles. See which one would most likely fit your ideas. We have already talked about consumer magazines and trade publications. Here are a few other magazine markets open to freelance writers.

Check the guidelines for denominational magazines. Some of them publish weekly and therefore need a lot of material. Others are monthly. Many distribute through churches rather than subscription so that gives you an idea of the readership.

Neighborhood magazines are usually looking for material about your city or one area of the city. Some cities have the Westside News, the Eastside News, the Southside News, and the Northside News. Some get even more specific and publish a newspaper for large neighborhoods. These markets may not be paying markets but people

Neighborhood Magazines
Written for a specific area of a town or city.

Regional Magazines
Serving a specific geographic region larger than a
town or group of towns.

State Magazines
Beautiful glossy publications that love news from
the communities they serve.

Denominational Magazines
Published by a specific group of believers who are associated
with a particular denomination.

will become familiar with your name and know you are a writer. As you build a platform, you can pitch to bigger markets and expand the reach of your influence. You are usually a little freer to talk about your books and other writing endeavors in these smaller publications.

Regional magazines are also good markets. These magazines serve a specific geographic territory but a bigger area than neighborhoods. Most states also have their own publications. Regional magazines and state magazine are noncompeting markets, which means they don't have the same readership. You could possibly publish your article one place and then offer it as a reprint to similar publications in different areas of the country.

Trade magazines cover topics relevant to the industry they serve. In most cases, you do not have to work in the industry to write for their magazines. Knowledge of the industry is a must so you can use the correct terminology and not write anything off base. If you think you'd like to write for trade magazines, you may be surprised to learn how many exist!

Consumer magazines are written with a broad viewpoint so they reach a wide audience. You see many of these magazines on newsstands, and you probably subscribe to some. They cover general interest topics and offer articles on a wide variety of subjects. Consumer magazines offer great opportunity for writers, but the competition is stiff for getting a publishing credit in one of those magazines. Don't forget, it is tough, not impossible. So, if that is your dream (as it is for many writers), keep trying.

Writers Groups

Writers groups are an excellent way to quickly immerse yourself in the writing culture. They offer instruction as well as encouragement to new writers. These groups often discuss good break-in markets and writing opportunities.

Check market guides if you are looking for a writers group. They usually have a listing in the back by state. Search online to see if you find mention of a writers group in your area. Talk to writers in your area to find out if they belong in a group.

If you can't find an established writers group in your area, start one. It doesn't take more than another person or two to get started. When the group is established, you can invite other people and advertise. Churches, libraries, and bookstores are both excellent places to meet.

Some people prefer online groups. These groups are similar to in-person groups but the members could be anywhere in the world. There are programs like Zoom on your computer which you can use to meet face to face. The group could also meet by email, but face-to-face gives you the opportunity to look at each other as you critique each other's work.

There are also some Facebook writers groups in place. These usually specialize in one type of writing and don't always include the critique element. They are very helpful, however, for networking and finding new writing gigs.

Determining Your Audience

Knowing your target audience increases your chance of making a sale with your article. It is called "target" audience because it is much like a target. You know what it looks like and where you want to hit it. But unless you know how to use your tools and aim proficiently, you miss the target and thereby have a less than successful attempt.

Knowing your target audience increases your chance of making a sale with your article.

Read the guidelines; look at the advertising in the magazine; determine the voice and tone of the articles. The audience of a periodical is specific. You can't write hoping someone of a different demographic will pick up your article and be thrilled.

Your target may be adults of a certain age, children, teens, tweens, or other specialty groups. As you write your article, especially when starting out, you may need to stop occasionally and ask yourself if what you have written is hitting your target or if you need to make any adjustments to come closer to the bull's eye.

Magazine, blog, and e-zine opportunities exist for every audience. Often your research can be used to write articles for different readers from one session of research. Use and reuse your research.

As you think of reusing your research, it is helpful to consider the different article formats you can use to present your information. Taking your research and creating different types of articles, blogs and e-zines, allows you to make the most of what you have learned through studying your subject.

Most people either love research or they don't. There doesn't seem to be much middle ground. Part of the anxiety about research is it is a lot of work and sometimes requires an enormous amount of digging through material to find the fact you are looking for. Some personalities thrive on the hunt for the perfect statistic or story. Others would be happy never to hear the word research and want to write from their realms of experience. But if you are going to write articles, you must learn the best ways to research so you can properly support your articles.

Query Letters

When you have chosen a topic you are passionate about, begin writing your query letter. The query letter is a question (query and question come from the same Latin root) or pitch to the editor about his or her interest in your subject and article. The query letter is an important piece of writing because it is your introduction to the editor. Through your query letter the editor can observe your writing style, see how you are going to handle the article, and learn a little about you. The query letter is your first impression piece so you need to make sure it is specific, complete, and polished. A poor query letter rarely leads to an invitation to submit an article.

Writers have differing opinions as to the best time to write a query letter. Of course, the writer can choose that time. Querying before you have completed your article saves time since you can be writing while the publisher is deciding whether to accept your idea. Querying early in the process can also give you the opportunity to tweak your material and slant to be a good fit for the specific magazine. The editor can also make suggestions so the article better fits his or her magazine.

> The query letter is a question or pitch to the editor about his or her interest in your subject and article.

New writers tend to wait until the article is finished before writing a query. The thought is *How can I possibly write a query letter about something I haven't even written yet?* For new writers, it is probably wise to do the first query or two this way. You can learn about the process and learn the different stages of querying and writing. As you become more comfortable and accomplished in the article writing process, you will also be able to skillfully craft a query before the article is written.

More experienced writers can easily write a query when an idea pops into his or her head and begins to germinate. They can write a query letter before the article is written. Experience teaches you how to offer an appealing slant to the editor, how to estimate word count, how many sources are needed, and so forth.

Postal mail used to be the only way to query and you had to supply a self-addressed stamped envelope. Now many publishers accept queries by email. Check the magazine's website and writers guidelines to see if e-queries are accepted. Using email is efficient for writers and publishers. You communicate easily without waiting for the post office to act as a middle man. However, don't compromise professionalism just because you are using email. Follow proper business letter format and protocol. The only difference in what you say and how you say it between an email query and a snail mail query is the method by which it is delivered. Be sure to respect the guidelines, and if a magazine still only accepts queries by mail, only use that method. Some magazine article guidelines also say they only accept complete manuscripts. In that case, you send the entire manuscript with a cover letter.

Your query letter should be addressed to a specific editor. Some guidelines may give you a name to query. Others say send to "Editor" and give you a physical or email address. When you encounter instructions to address your query to "Editor," do some research to find out the name of the editor who oversees the type of article you are offering. Publishing house websites are not always up to date but can be helpful. Ask another writer who writes for the same publication if he or she has information to share. You can call the telephone number of the publishing house and ask the receptionist if he or she can give you the name of the editor of the section you want to submit to. Make sure you have the correct spelling and title. If the name is Pat Smith or Chris Matthews or another name used for either a man or a woman, try to find out the gender so you can use the correct prefix. A picture of the editor sometimes accompanies the guidelines. If not drop the title and say "Dear Pat Smith."

Parts of a Query Letter

Since query letters should be no more than one page, you should organize your material and present it in both a succinct and creative way.

If you are a new writer, you may feel like a lengthy introduction of who you are and what you do is necessary and the way to start your query. However, unless you have national/international name recognition, your name and who you are is not as important to an editor considering your work as is whether you can write. He or she will be the judge of your writing skills based on your query letter.

EXPERT WORD

Spelling the name correctly and having the correct title for the editor is really important. When I was an editor having either one of those things wrong was grounds for rejecting the query.
Larry J. Leech II, former magazine editor now an author and writing coach. www.larryleech.com

The first paragraph is your hook. You want to hook your editor from the very beginning just as you need to hook your reader. The same paragraph could be used in both places. We discuss more about the hook of your article in Chapter 8. But as you write your query, concentrate on making sure you grab the editor's attention with your hook.

You may think to yourself *The hook is the first paragraph of my article. How do you write a hook for a query?* These two hooks—the one for your query and the one for your article, are written the same way with the same purpose. In many cases, they are interchangeable. If you haven't written your article yet and take time to write a hook for your query, you may be able to use that same hook for the start of your article. There are many different types of hooks.

Anecdotes draw your reader into the article. An anecdote is a short story of interest and leads your reader to the subject of the article. This anecdote can be a personal story, something historical, or a retelling of something you have experienced or heard.

Statistics work well as hooks. Usually the more startling the better. Something to cause your reader to think.

Quotes also work well as starting points for articles.

Questions create effective hooks. Asking a thoughtful question can make the reader (and editor) see the value of your article as the answer for the question.

The first paragraph showcases your writing and should entice the editor to read on. If he or she immediately sees you can present your ideas in a way sure to reach his or her readers, reading on is a sure thing. When the editor sees you can draw the reader in to the article with an eye-catching hook, he or she asks for more of your writing.

The second paragraph should contain the title of the article, the length of the article, how you will develop the subject, sources you might use such as books or interviews, the takeaway for that specific magazine's readership, when the article will be available, and any other important facts. If you have photos available to go with the article, state that here. Know why your article is a good fit for this market. Learn all you can about the publication, website, or blog before you query. If you can mention something to let the editor know you are familiar with the publication, this is a good place. A simple statement about enjoying a recent article suffices. You could also state how your article fits in with the focus of the magazine.

Your title should be catchy but not cute. Study the magazine you are submitting to and see what kind of titles they use. Are they straight informational? Do they draw the reader in? What is the average length? Can you find a tie-in in the news or on the calendar?

Make the editor's job easy by providing everything he or she needs to produce an eye-catching and exciting article fitting his or her readership. This paragraph is so important. When an editor knows you are interviewing good subjects, understand how to develop an article meaningful to the reader, are going way beyond what is necessary by providing sidebars, hot boxes, and photos, and can meet deadlines, you are much closer to a sale.

One frequent question is "Well, if I haven't written the article, how do I know how long it should be?"

The answer is simple. Study the guidelines for the magazine. The guidelines say the magazine is looking for articles 800-1000 words. You have not started your article yet. When you write it, write 900 words. Then you have some wiggle room if you go over your goal or miss it by a few words. You can confidently put your word count into your query when you know how long the acceptable limits of the word count are. The editor will not hold you to the exact count. You just need to make sure your word count is close to your proposed length. Don't propose an article of 1500 words to a magazine or website that is looking for 800-1000. That error will bring a quick reply to your query—rejection!

EXPERT WORD

Before you submit anything to a magazine editor, study the publication in print (or at least online) AND the magazine guidelines. My tip sounds obvious, but you would be shocked how many writers don't do this basic work. They send inappropriate articles or articles way over or under the expected word limits. Every magazine has a specific target reader. In the magazine and the guidelines, the editors are telling you their expectations. If you meet these needs, you will be way ahead of the other writers trying to get published in the magazine.

W. Terry Whalin, former magazine editor and published in more than 50 magazines, currently an acquisitions editor at Morgan James Publishing and the author of more than 60 books including *Book Proposals That Sell.*

The third paragraph should contain pertinent personal information and what qualifies you to write this article. You don't necessarily have to have educational degrees or specialized training.

The qualifying factor for you to write this article may be your life experiences. For example, you are writing an article titled "7 Ways to Keep Peace in the Family." You may not have a PhD. in counseling. You may have 11 children and much experience in keeping peace in your household. This article could be a serious article or a humorous piece. Regardless of the slant, your experience is your credential making you qualified to write this article. If you have writing experience, you can mention it here. If you are new to writing and don't have any writing credits, don't mention that. Let your writing speak for itself.

The fourth paragraph should thank the editor for taking time to read your query and state you look forward to hearing from him or her soon.

Some people like to query more than one topic at a time. There are pros and cons to that method. Especially when you are starting out, only send one at a time. Sometimes editors can be overwhelmed by too many choices. It's not likely you would be invited to send more than one article for an issue so propose your strongest idea. Then you can send another query later.

Remember when you are writing a query letter—

- Study the magazine to make sure your article is a good fit.

- Keep it short.

- Make it strong.

- Put your best "foot" forward (check for spelling errors, etc.).

- Single space and leave a line space between paragraphs.

Sample of a Successful Query Letter

(If you have a personal letterhead you can use it here instead of the list below.)

Name
Address
City and Zip
Phone
Website

Dear Editor (Remember not to say editor but address your letter to a person),

Often the difference between a good, informative article and an excellent article with pizzazz is on-site research. Becoming a "temporary expert" on a subject can put a real zing! in your article.

My article, "Become A Temporary Expert," includes stories of writers who have stepped into the shoes of a person, profession, or character he or she is writing about. This 1200-word article uses the round-up format to spotlight writers who have had success with this method. Also, briefly mentioned are other methods of research which are necessary even with the on-the-job research. For example, background reading, interviewing, attending lectures, etc.

Would your magazine be interested in this article? I could have it to you within twelve weeks of receiving a favorable reply.

Sincerely,
Author

AUTHOR NOTE

When I first started writing, I bought a book with templates and examples of every kind of document you might need as a writer. There were examples of fiction queries, nonfiction queries, article format, synopsis format. For a long time, I wrote my queries with the book open to the query example closest to what I needed. That book served me well and now falls open to the page with the magazine article query!

Sample of a Positive Reply to an Email Query

(This reply will likely be an email from the editor with a cut and paste of your query.)

Many email queries are answered by simply copying the query and adding a few additional notes. For example:

Thank you for your proposal. We would be glad to consider, on speculation, the following (please note the deadline and word count):

Issue 50—release date Jan 30   (This particular magazine lists the issue and publication date with every query response.)

"You Can Be a Public Speaker" (This was the query.)

Many surveys indicate public speaking is in the top three of fears. Public speaking?

Much of that fear is generated from lack of knowledge of how to be a public speaker. Some people are more comfortable than others speaking in public, but everyone can learn to broaden their knowledge and confidence in that area.

My 1,200-word article, "You Can Be a Public Speaker," gives five reasons we should equip ourselves to speak in public and five ways to be prepared when asked to speak. Anecdotes from speakers will be used as examples and Acts 13:19 will be used as a premise for this article – "If anyone has a word of encouragement for the people, please speak."

On Speculation means the editor agrees to look at your completed article, but until he or she reads the article will not guarantee publication and offer a contract.

Because this article was pitched to a magazine the author writes for regularly, this pitch did not require a bio. There was already a good relationship with the editor and when he saw the email address he recognized it as from someone he knows and whose work he is familiar with.

Remember to do your "homework" before submitting. Editors say a large number of the queries they receive are easy rejections. Why? Because the writers have not read the guidelines or studied the magazine and the article is not appropriate and does not fit their magazines. That should rarely happen if writers study the market they are submitting to and become familiar with the voice and slant of the magazine. Don't let yours be an easy rejection. Do your homework!

Pitching in Person

Occasionally you have the opportunity to meet editors at writers conferences. This gives you the chance to pitch ideas face-to-face. A meeting with an editor at a conference usually lasts ten or fifteen minutes and serves as your query if you pitch an idea. Your conversation can discuss slant, whether or not the magazine has published anything similar and when, and if the magazine might be interested in your topic. If you receive some interest in your article idea, the editor will give you specific guidelines or tell you where they are available. When you get that information and you hear the words, "Send it to me. I would love to take a look," you have the green light to write and/or polish your article and send it along. Just remember to make sure your article is the very best it can be before sending it, especially if this is for an editor you have never worked with before. Getting overly excited about the "green light" may make you careless because you want to hurry and send it. Unless the editor says, "I would like it on my desk next week," and that is not likely, take the time to make sure your article is the very best it can be before you push the send button. Just be reasonable about the time you take. You don't want the editor to forget about your conversation!

Keep in mind when this happens, the invitation is only for the editor to take a look on speculation. In other words, it is not a guarantee of publication, but a willingness to seriously consider your work. If you follow the guidelines and heed the advice of the editor, you have a good chance of your article being accepted. He or she has already expressed interest so you have crossed the first hurdle.

Make the most of a meeting with an editor by being prepared. Know what his or her magazine publishes. Study what the focus is and if they do special themes. Make a list of article ideas to fit the magazine's focus so you will not waste valuable meeting time. When you meet the editor, keep personal introductions brief. Make the most of your time to pitch your idea or ideas. If you have planned properly, you may be able to pitch more than one idea.

An editor will not invite you to send your manuscript unless he or she is serious. When the invitation has been given, don't forfeit the chance to get your work on the editor's desk. Ask the editor for a business card so you have the correct email. The card is also useful for sending the editor a thank you note for sharing his or her expertise at your meeting. File your business cards in a place you can easily retrieve them when you want to contact him or her with another query.

AUTHOR NOTE

As a melancholy, introverted personality, I was happy writing a query letter and pitching my article without a face-to-face meeting. Then I began attending conferences and didn't want to miss an opportunity to meet with the editors and publishers who were present. In the beginning the most difficult question was, "What do you write?" I didn't know exactly what I wrote, had no idea my genre was, or how to effectively pitch my work.

It helped me to write my introduction and a brief synopsis of my work. If I practiced before the meeting and was comfortable getting started, I found the meeting went more smoothly thereafter.

Getting ready for a meeting with an editor

You can become very nervous at your first meeting or two with an editor. Here are a few helpful hints to make it go more smoothly. Just make sure you don't put the editor, publisher, or freelance writer you are meeting with up on a pedestal. They are doing their jobs looking for writers just like you are doing yours to sell your work.

Pitch—Presenting your work to a prospective editor or publisher

Know what you want to say. Write out your 30-second introduction of yourself and then a brief synopsis of the article you are pitching. Read them aloud in front of a mirror over and over until you are comfortable. You don't have to memorize every word, but if you are familiar with what you want to say you can speak clearly and at ease. Pick the strongest phrases to hook the editor and lead with those.

Choose your editor or publisher carefully. Do your homework and study the magazines, blogs, or websites of editors you have the opportunity to meet. Familiarity with their publications allows you to know whether or not their publication is a good fit for you. Often the magazines, blogs, or websites you read frequently are a good place to start. You are already familiar with the style and voice of the magazine.

Record all your conversations and meetings with professionals in a notebook. When you attend a conference, there are many, many people you are likely to meet, talk to, and pitch. You think you couldn't possibly forget which editor asked you to send your completed article to him or her or which one offered to let you write a column for a specific magazine, but when you get home all your conversations may seem to run together. So, to avoid any problems with forgetting or mixing things up, take a notebook to every meeting. If you know of people you want to meet with, study their publication ahead of time and think through possible ideas to pitch.

Relax. (You are probably thinking—What? How can I relax when I am going to talk to a real, live editor?) If you have prepared and are ready to pitch, you will be fine. Sit down just as you were meeting a new friend. Smile and introduce yourself. Don't use a lot of your time exchanging pleasantries, though. If it is a scheduled appointment you only have ten or fifteen minutes during which to pitch your idea or ideas. Don't waste precious minutes discussing the weather, family, or travel fiascoes unless they are pertinent to what you are pitching. If it is not a scheduled meeting and you just happen to ride the elevator with someone you had been hoping to pitch to, you probably have only 30 seconds to initiate a conversation. Hopefully if the editor is interested, he or she continues the conversation when you both step out of the elevator.

Don't be afraid of pauses. Sometimes the editor or publisher must think through your idea and how it fits in upcoming issues. Don't get nervous about the silence and think you must say something. Just silently pray the idea is well-received until the editor is ready to comment.

Make sure to exchange business cards at all meetings, whether scheduled or chance. Business cards don't have to be fancy or expensive, but they do need to contain current information. It is also a good idea to include your photo on your card. Editors and publishers attend many conferences and talk to scores of people and it is helpful to be able to quickly match a name with a face.

Always remember to send a thank you to anyone you met with. Why? You may think ten or fifteen minutes doesn't warrant a thank you note, but you are wrong. The person you met with has given you advice, direction, and maybe even an opportunity to have your work published. Also, you want to build relationships with everyone in the publishing industry and these meetings are a good place to start. Thanking the editor or publisher for his or her time gives you another chance to connect. Handwritten notes are nice and probably garner more attention than email ones, but email is acceptable. One good thing about sending an email note is you then have a presence in the editor's email box.

Sample Verbal Pitch

Hello, Mr. Smith (editor). How are you?" Reaches out to shake hands.

"Fine. Thank you. Have a seat." Motions to empty chair across from him.

"My name is Darah Jones. I enjoy reading your magazine, and I have an idea I think may be a good fit."

Mr. Smith nods. "What's your idea?"

"I have just completed a trip into the jungle studying the mating habits of glass frogs. Since you recently ran an article about electric eels, I thought perhaps this might be a good follow up for the water animal lovers in your audience. I notice you spotlight at least one extreme creature in every issue."

"You're right. I don't believe we have ever featured glass frogs. How you would develop that."

"While on my trip I visited a jungle lab where they were studying the glass frogs. It was fascinating since I could observe their organs as they moved around, ate, and did other things."

"Do you have any high res photos?"

"Oh, yes. I am a camera bug and loved having such an unusual subject to photograph."

"Darah, I'd love to see your article on speculation. Could you email it to me?"

"Of course."

"And don't forget to send the photos as well."

"I will." Standing up Darah says, "Thank you very much."

Darah was elated the editor had given her a positive response to her verbal query. She saved the time of crafting a written query and could now work on her article to send to this editor. Before she starts work on her article, she should write a thank you note to the editor for meeting with her and listening to her pitch about her article. She should have the editor's contact information from the card she picked up from the meeting table.

Rejection

Many people don't like to hear the word "rejection." They feel it is a rejection of them as a person. Article rejection is not personal. Magazines are business and sometimes must reject an article because it doesn't fit the business model. While the immediate result for writers may seem negative, if you can adjust your attitude about this one word, the writing world seems a little more inviting.

Some writers don't use the word rejection. They prefer to consider a rejection as a "No, thank you." That perspective is much more positive and true. The editor is not rejecting you as a writer, he or she is only rejecting this piece of writing, often because it doesn't fit the magazine or because he or she has published a similar subject recently.

One comment often seen on rejection letters is "Does not fit our editorial needs." Although this seems like a one size fits all rejection, it is not. Most magazines have an editorial calendar and stick closely to it. So, it is easy to determine if an article fits or not.

Don't lose heart when you receive a rejection. Rejection is a big part of getting published. And writers at all stages of their careers receive rejection. When you receive a rejection, if there are any comments on your manuscript take them seriously. Work on the problem areas. If an editor says, "Does not meet our editorial needs, but we would like to see more of your work," get busy and come up with a fresh article. Query them and begin by thanking them for their response to your query about "_____" and asking to see more. Tell them you are sending another idea for consideration and appreciate their taking time to read it. It may take several queries to break in to a market but with each one you should come closer to hitting your target market.

Cover Letter

Cover letter is another term you hear regarding articles. Cover letters and query letters are not the same thing. A query letter is written to open the door for your manuscript. A cover letter accompanies your manuscript.

A cover letter is not used with articles as much as it is with books. But there are times when one is necessary. One such time would be for Darah Jones in the scenario of her meeting with an editor. The editor

A query letter is written to open the door for your manuscript. A cover letter accompanies your manuscript.

gave her a verbal go-ahead to send her manuscript so she does not need to write a query letter.

When Darah sends her manuscript to the editor, she needs to include a cover letter. A cover letter is brief and serves as a reminder to the editor that he or she had spoken with Darah about her manuscript. If this meeting was at a writers conference, Darah might start her cover letter with a sentence like this. "It was a pleasure meeting you at the Superior Writers Conference last month."

If you have sent a query to the magazine and received a positive reply, you might start out this way. "Thank you for your positive response to my query…"

If you have previously sent the article and the editor requested changes, you may start this way. "enclosed is my article, NAME OF ARTICLE, with requested revisions."

If you are communicating with the editor by email, the email can serve as your cover letter.

When you attend writers conferences you will probably observe several different approaches to editors. Here are a few of them.

Aggressive Agnes. She is the one you see doing everything she can to get to the front of the line so she can meet an editor and pitch her work. She has little concern as to whether or not she pushes someone out of the way as she jockeys for the best position. At meals, she may move purses and briefcases next to the editor so she can have the best seat. Agnes is not patient and doesn't want to wait until her time for a specified appointment with the editor. She is going to make that encounter happen. Do you want the editor to remember you as an Agnes?

Sam Stalker. Sam appears everywhere his targeted editor is. Sam makes sure to be in the classes, waiting until the editor is ready to leave after class then positions himself to walk down the same hall at the same time. Sam has even been known to follow an editor to the restroom for an extra captive moment. The editor is appalled at how Sam appears at everywhere corner. You probably don't want to be labeled as a Sam either.

Peaceful Paula. Paula is patient and waits her turn to speak with her targeted editor. She makes an appointment and is prepared and on time for their meeting. She is friendly in the hall when passing the editor but respects the time when the editor may needs a few minutes to himself or herself. Paula's quiet yet professional manner is memorable to the editor she is meeting with.

You want the first meeting with an editor to be memorable in a good way. You must be

Professional,

Businesslike,

Polite,

Prepared,

Respectful,

Appreciative.

Chapter 6
Research

We have discussed the benefit of doing research for more than one article at a time and the importance of a good filing system. How do you research? What is the best way to find information? Are there others who can help you? Why is research important?

Let's start at the beginning. Research is important, especially for articles written to inform readers about a new subject. Few people know everything about all subjects and need some help with background facts if nothing else. Articles are made stronger by the use of quotes, statistics, or case studies pertaining to your subject. Never assume because a fact comes to mind and you must have learned it in school or somewhere else, that it is correct. Always fact check. Even if you know a lot about your subject, having a credible source other than yourself gives validly to what you are writing.

As you begin your research, remember you may need to document the source for facts, quotations, and other information not considered common knowledge. The best way is to save proper documentation as you go.

When you find a quote, fact, or other piece of information you need, put all the details of where you got the information in a special folder in your computer or file in your office. If the information is from a book, make a copy of the book title page, copyright page, and the page where you found something to use in your article. Document an article similarly, copying the cover and article pages. Then file it somewhere until you are ready to submit your finished manuscript. Some publishers request a copy of the list with submission and others just want you to keep it until you need it.

Footnotes and endnotes are not needed if you give credit in your text for the source of your information.

For example, instead of writing "Communication is important, but we sometimes forget it involves two elements—speaking and listening"[1] and then having to provide a footnote or end note telling you where the quote comes from, why not do it this way. In their book *Words to Live By*, Linda Gilden and Dalene Parker remind us "communication is important but we sometimes forget it involves two elements—speaking and listening." The last way eliminates the footnote or endnote and gives you the information about the source right with the quote. This allows your readers immediate information and excludes the need to turn somewhere else to find the source of the quote.

Many of you were taught in school to footnote everything—good practice keeping track of your research and give proper attribution. As an author, you have to learn the preferred way of magazine editors.

Another offshoot of your research is that as you peruse the materials others have written, you will no doubt see many different formats and arrangements of material. As you see unusual layouts or a new way of doing something, you can make note and someday incorporate them into your own writing. Your research may also spawn additional ideas. Jot them down in your ideas folder and you will never wonder what to write about.

Years ago, when you wanted to research a subject you picked up your paper and pen and went to the local library to spend the day or maybe longer. You may have also included a side trip to the book store or a university or college library. You looked for local people to interview to "pick their brains."

Life changed quickly with the introduction of home computers. The Internet gives you access to the world and information is at your fingertips. Research methods no longer require a trip away from home. You can sit at your computer at any time of day in your pajamas and learn facts about any subject at all.

Keep in mind as you work, you utilize the system of organization you have in place. Many people rely solely on their computers for storing and organizing material. Some still prefer the paper and filing method. Some use a combination of both. Find the system you are comfortable with and stick with it.

As you write your article and your creative juices are flowing you are probably going to find other ideas popping into your brain as you work. Don't let that sidetrack you. Make a file titled "Ideas" and when a new idea comes to mind, jot it down for later. That releases it from your brain and helps you stay focused on your immediate project.

Before you start your research, make an outline of your article and what you would like to cover. Keep in mind word count so you don't over plan. Remember this outline is just a temporary guideline and you can add or subtract to it if you don't follow "rabbit trails." Rabbit trails are tangents a writer tends to add into his or her writing which are distracting to the main point of the article and do nothing to support the point of the article.

Here are suggestions for ways to research your article subjects.

Read, Read, Read

If you are an avid reader, research is probably something you enjoy. Readers usually love learning new things and discovering information. Books, other magazine articles, newspapers, and the like are great sources of information. When you are researching a subject for a possible article, get a small notebook before you start and designate it as your research notebook. Then as you read, make notes of anything you might possibly use and the location of the information. This may seem like a lot to do when you are just in the research stage, however, it will be time well spent. If you ever need to go back and find a resource, you have information as to how to do find it easily and without having to start looking for it all over again.

Libraries

The local library is still a great source of research yet often underused. Some people think of the library as a big building filled with books and if they don't need a book, they don't need to go to the library. Libraries not only house books but also have historical journals, magazine articles on microfilm, and research librarians, who should be a writer's best friend. You can go to a library and spend hours studying the books, looking through microfilm, reading periodicals from many years back.

Libraries are filled with books, magazines, newspapers, market research, and many other forms of print information. They subscribe to hundreds of magazines. So, when you begin to write and look for possible markets for your work, you can just camp out in a comfy chair in the periodical section and browse for hours. Make sure you have a notebook to record possible markets, the editor's name, website, and submission policy. Look in the book section and find one or two books you think might be helpful. Go sit in front of the shelf where you find it. Other similar books are shelved in the same place and should give you additional information. Your Research Librarian is familiar with all these. He or she is willing to help you find information you need and can point you to resources you weren't aware of. Sometimes this resource, your librarian, is overlooked.

Another library "gold mine" are the thousands and thousands of articles they have on microfilm. You may have to go sit in the archives section and search through many different articles, but having that option is valuable when you are researching events or people from long ago. Look in the periodical guide, which has a list of articles by year and the publications they appeared in.

With the Internet, you not only have access your local library from your home, but you also have the capability of accessing many libraries across the country online. Many local libraries participate in a lending system with other libraries and can get books and information for you quickly.

Not all libraries offer online access. Check with your local library and find out what they offer online. Local libraries often give you the capability to search their card catalogs, see what is in their reference sections, and, during business hours, have a live chat with a librarian to receive her help. Local libraries can also provide access to libraries all over your state and beyond. Usually your library card number gets you into your library's website.

Your library is a great source of research. Don't overlook it.

EXPERT WORD

A few other possible helps found in your local library:

A local history and genealogy department, with a separate collection of books and local records (primary sources) stretching back to the 1800s when our library was founded. In addition to these hard-copy resources, we also have the microfilms mentioned above. A number of art installations and galleries.

Meeting rooms and study rooms for writers needing a quiet space to work (with free Wi-Fi).

Tons of Online resources, including scholarly databases like Academic Search Premier, Discus, and digital downloads for books, music and e-books (all free to access from home with your library card number), Digital Access to New York Times dating back to the 1850s, digital access to agriculture and census records... the list goes on. To browse these offerings, you can go to your library's website and click the "go to research" and "go to resources" tabs. There are a lot of good subscriptions.

Libraries have lots of programs, some of which have community experts from different

fields come share their knowledge. For example, before the eclipse, they brought in a Wofford College Physics and Astronomy professor to do a presentation.

Not all libraries have all this, but the field as a whole is moving in the "We're more than just books!" direction.

Susanne Parker, librarian at the Spartanburg, SC Public Library

The Internet

Back in the fifties, the first computers took up more than an entire room in the average size house. Just two decades later, computers had been scaled down to a size that worked in the home without requiring an enormous amount of space. Since that time, the actual devices have gotten smaller and smaller and and more functional.

With the advent of computers came the introduction of the Internet. Within seconds you could be connected to information all over the world. In December of 1995, according to internetworldstats. com, there were 16 million users of the internet which was 0.4% of the world population. Now, over two decades later in June of 2017, there were 3,885 million users which amounted to 51.7% of the world's population.

For writers, the growth of the Internet continues to open doors and make information more accessible. As a means of research, the Internet allows writers to connect with experts, find the latest statistics, and learn about places they could never travel to.

Searches often yield millions of sites providing information relative to what you search for. Occasionally you don't get as many. If you feel like there are other sources or you don't get the information you are looking for, rearrange your words in the search box or ask a question another way. Soon, you should have plenty of information for your article.

When you put your subject into the search bar, if it is more than one word, put quotation marks around it to have the search engine keep it together. Quotation marks let the search engine know you are searching for a phrase, not a word. Without the quotation marks the search engine gives you many options for each word in the phrase. Quotation marks narrow your search. Also think of other synonyms or similar subjects so you can spread your research out even further. Visit sites that look interesting from your search and pay attention to the ads and articles in the side panels of the site. These often yield pertinent information on a subject. If you are searching for information on a specific person, you can also search for family members or organizations they are associated with to find stories to support your article.

Some people are led to believe if it is on the Internet, it has to be fact. Not always so. Some sites allow anyone to post information so it could be what you read is hearsay.

The worldwide web opened a new horizon for writers. Research can be done quickly and easily on most any subject. Type your subject in your search bar and you have a plethora of information at your fingertips. Often one site leads to another and you can go as deep in your research as you would like.

A word of caution here. When you are using the web for research, make sure you go all the way back to the original source. Many sites contain information they took from other sites. And sometime in the transfer of material the source is sited incorrectly. Websites should provide you with the original source so you can go back to it for verification. The original source is called the primary source. Publishers much prefer you use the original or primary source

> When you are using the web for research, make sure you go all the way back to the original source.

This requirement is particularly true when using quotes. If someone uses an original quote from someone else in a speech, paper, or article, it can be mistaken for the author's words. The importance of integrity in your writing is huge and reflects how the rest of your material is received.

A word about Wikipedia. Many people go first to this site when they want information. Though you can find lots of information on this site, it is not necessarily the best place to go because anyone can change or post material regardless of their credentials. Check the resources cited at the bottom of the Wikipedia pages and go to the sources. Often that takes you quickly to the original information. Some magazines and newspapers do not accept Wikipedia as a source for your articles because of the reasons stated above.

Email

Email also provides a way for you to contact experts and ask questions of them. If your subject is in any way academic, you can contact heads of departments and professors at colleges and universities with questions about your subject. You can conduct interviews through email. Prepare a list of questions you would like to address. Be sure to state it is not necessary to answer all questions, but any questions he or she can speak to will be appreciated.

There are pros and cons to using email for interviews. The pros include it is easy, you don't have to travel to conduct the interview, there is no expense, the expert can answer questions any time of night or day, you have the answers written down by the expert so there is no mixing up of information. Some of the cons are you don't have the opportunity to ask follow-up questions, you don't have the opportunity to observe the surroundings of the interviewee, when you submit the questions you can't add to them, you miss the face-to-face element.

AUTHOR NOTE

When I was writing my book, *Love Notes in Lunchboxes*, I wanted to find an expert who would say notes of encouragement would have long term positive effects on your children. I entered my question and asked for educators or psychologists to respond.

I only received one reply. "I am not the expert. I am the secretary for an expert. But for years I wrote notes to put in my daughter's lunchbox. I actually have saved them all and would be glad to share them with you."

This lady turned out to be a gold mine of information. She introduced me to her daughter in another state who was very helpful. Her daughter even offered to send me her prized shoebox of notes she had in her closet.

Even though I didn't get the exact response I was after from an expert, these ladies were perfect help for my project and even helped me on my next book, *Love Notes on His Pillow*.

Don't know any experts? Search for websites on the subject you are researching and see who the authors of the articles are. See if they provide an email. Look in the front of books to see who wrote the foreword. There may be enough information to find the author.

Search on profnet.com. You must register as a journalist, but registration is free. Then you have access to information from experts all over the world. When you go to the site, you see a series of drop-down boxes allowing you to post a question, state the type of expert you are seeking, whether or not you want someone in a certain geographic location, etc. Within about 24 hours you receive replies from (usually) many sources with great information about your subject. Just don't forget to give them credit.

Interviews

We have discussed interviews a bit when we talked about profile articles, but there is more important information about writing an interview article.

Interviews are one of the most enjoyable forms of research. You meet with someone who is an expert of the subject and can give you lots of information often with a new perspective. Using quotes from another individual brings credibility to your article and reinforces what you already know.

When using interviews as a form of research, plan carefully for your time with the expert. You are not looking for his or her life story. You are looking for one or two gems to give your article an extra boost in credibility and step it up to the next level. Before the interview, whether it is an in-person visit or a telephone conversation, decide what type of information you are looking for. What area of your subject could this person speak best to? How could a few comments from this person elevate the interview from good to best? Set up a reasonable time length as well as a time to meet.

Read everything you can about the person. If he or she has written books, read them. If there are other interviews on file, read them. When you become familiar with the person you interview and have a good idea of his or her background and how the story fits in your article, you can craft a list of questions to help you make the most of your time. Don't use your interview time to have the subject answer questions you already know the answer to. You want to dig and find a gem of information to make your article stand out and sparkle.

EXPERT WORD

Great interviewers know what they don't need to get out of an interview.

Don't ask questions you can find the answers to on your own. Spend your preparation time gathering readily available common knowledge so you can focus on personal and unique content during the interview.

Ask permission to record the session then lead off with open-ended questions. "What's your opinion on...?" Or, "Please share your thoughts concerning..." this allows the subject to share from his or her heart. Let them share as much as they want, as you listen, nod, and don't interrupt. Add in your common data to give your article balance.

Linda Goldfarb author, freelance writer, communication coach, and veteran talk-radio host.
www.LivePowerfullyNow.com/coaching

If you plan to cover the person's entire life, you probably are thinking about a profile article rather than just using this person as part of your research for a subject article.

When you are looking for someone to interview about your article, check in your area first since you have an automatic connection. Check business, service providers, local newspapers, and educational institutions. Often college and university heads of departments or great resources for articles.

Face-to-Face Interviews

The best way to conduct an interview is face-to-face. Not only can you see facial expressions, but you can also observe body language, the personal surroundings of the person, and facial expressions. If it is not convenient for you to go to them, take care when choosing a place to meet. Restaurants seem to be the logical spot, but they are often noisy and have lots of distractions.

AUTHOR NOTE

I once wrote a series of articles on family reunions. I had researched books and newspaper and magazine articles to find information about special places for reunions and important aspects of planning. In the front of one of the books I found at the library, a name that had become familiar on the subject of family reunions surfaced yet again as the writer of the foreword. Under her name was the name of the university where she was chairman of the Family Reunion Department. I had no idea any university had a whole department dedicated to family reunions. I called the university and asked to speak to this person and had a very enlightening and helpful conversation. It only took a few minutes of her time and she was very gracious to speak to me right on the spot. That isn't always possible and you may have to make an appointment, but for me it worked this time!

Coffee shops work if they are off the beaten path and not during their busiest time of the day. Libraries often have small study rooms or lounges where you can go and have privacy as well as quiet. Be sure to take a digital recorder and with your subject's permission, record your time together. However, be sure to test your recorder before you go, insert fresh batteries, and make sure it downloads to your computer. If it doesn't have this feature, you spend a lot of time transcribing. Prepare a list of questions ahead of time to keep you on track and remind you of your focus. You may deviate from the list, but it is a good way to get started and keep the interview moving in the direction of your goal.

Prepare to record the conversation. This frees you from having to make sure you note everything said and allows you to relax more during the conversation. Take note of the important phrases so you can go back to them on the recorder. Digital recorders work well and many can transfer recordings to your computer.

Be respectful of the time of the person you are interviewing. If you asked for an hour of their time, don't exceed the time by even a minute. If you have asked for only thirty minutes, take just that. If the person you are interviewing invites you to chat longer, stay if you like. If not, thank him or her for the interview and quickly say your good-byes. Before you leave, ask if you may call with further questions or clarification of something that was said. Always remember to write a thank you note and get it in the mail as soon as possible but within a week of the interview. When your article comes out, mail a copy to the person with another short thanks.

If you are unable to meet in person, suggest an online face-to-face chat. At least when you see each other you can exchange nonverbal communication through your body language and facial expressions.

Telephone Interviews

Telephone interviews often work best when you are seeking expert quotes. For one thing, you are not limited to people in your geographic area. You can pick up the phone and reach people anywhere in the world. So, take advantage of the telephone when you just want a few sentences or a paragraph to back up your other research.

If face-to-face interviews are not possible, ask if you could have ten or fifteen minutes on the telephone. Have your questions prepared ahead of time. For a telephone interview, you may want to send the questions to your subject so he or she has had time to think about the answers. Here again, be respectful of time and don't go over what was agreed upon. Remember proper thanks just as if you were meeting in person.

E-mail Interviews

Interviews can also be done online without any visual contact with your subject. First, make contact and request the interview. Explain how it works and how you would like to proceed. Give your subject a short synopsis of your goal for the article and how he or she can help. After the initial contact and agreement, prepare a list of questions you would like answered. Be very specific so there is no confusion. Give your subject any parameters you would like to have in place. Give the freedom to ignore a question or two for any reason. Then give a deadline of when you would like to have the answers returned. In many ways, email is a great way to conduct an interview. You already have the questions and answers in writing, and there will be no mistake about what was said.

Email questions can be answered by several experts in the field at the same time. They can each reply on their schedules when they have a few moments free. If you don't know the person, you need to include a paragraph of introduction and how you connected with them in your article.

Here are a few suggested questions to use when interviewing. Many questions focus on the subject of your article. But a few general questions allow you to get to know your subject better and often lead to information right on target.

1. How did you come to your present position?

2. Why did you choose this career field?

3. What was your most embarrassing moment in life?

4. Who would you like to spend a morning with (past or present)?

5. If you could have dinner with one person alive or dead, who would that be?

6. What was the most fun activity you did in the last year?

7. What do you do to relax?

8. Are you a person of faith? How does that affect your life/business?

9. What do you think is a person's greatest attribute?

10. If you could go back and talk to yourself at age 18, what would you say?

11. What person in your life has had the most influence on you?

No matter what form of interviewing you use, be sure to be considerate of your subject in every way. Do not overstay your allotted time. Ask what title the person prefers before or after the name and how he or she would like the name to appear.

One thing that may come up in a discussion about the article is the draft. Some people you interview will ask to see the article before you send it to the magazine. Your magazine may have a specific policy about that so you must check with the magazine before you agree to allow it. If the magazine doesn't have a policy about it, you must use your judgment. In most cases, this is probably not a good idea. Why? Because the article is printed in draft form and the person looks at it, they are likely to say things like, "Well, this is what I said, but I think I would like to say it a different way." Or "I'd like to add something to this paragraph here." Or "Yes, that is the way I looked when I said it but I didn't mean to smirk." Those types of questions are likely to come up when people look at a yet-to-be-submitted article and cost you extra time and often quite a bit of work. Sometimes the subject wants you to do almost a total rewrite. If there is a reason you think your subject should have a look at the article before you submit, then allow that. Just be cautious and take all possibilities into consideration.

EXPERT WORD

Always be ready with a question no matter where you are.

I was at a meeting where several high-profile speakers were on the program. At the end there were several minutes left and the emcee said, "Does anyone have a question?" I couldn't think of one to ask.

From then on, I made sure I had a question no matter where I was. As communicators, we should be able to engage in conversation anywhere. Now I always have something to talk about and that has been beneficial, especially if I am seated at a dinner with people I don't know. I have often met interesting people just by talking to them at dinner, the doctor's office. Later I can ask for an interview so I can tell their interesting stories.

Some of my favorite questions are

What's the funniest thing that's happened to you in your job?

How has your faith impacted your writing? I was interviewing Richard Paul Evans one time and when I asked that question he immediately perked up. No one has ever asked me that question before," he said. "I would love to talk about my faith."

What is something you would like to tell people?

Peggy Sue Wells, author of 28 books including *Rediscovering Your Happily Ever After,* and *Slavery in the Land of the Free.*

Remember when preparing for an interview:

- Choose a quiet place. Avoid noisy restaurants and coffee shops.
- Meet on your subject's territory, if possible.
- Read all you can about the person you are interviewing before you go.
- Prepare a list of questions.
- Have more questions than you have time.
- Stick to the time frame you have requested.
- Record your session but take notes as well.
- Take your camera if you need photos of your subject.
- Ask how the person would like his or her name listed in the attribution.
- Don't forget your manners—verbally thank him or her when you finish and send a written thank you note when you get home.
- Send a copy of the published article, even if you have just used a quote or two.

Museums

If your article is historical in nature, you may want to visit museums to learn more about your subject. Seeing the artifacts and historical items gives you a visual to write from; your information comes alive in your mind and your reader's mind. Often the curator is a great source of information and willing to help.

Chapter 7
Types of Articles

Personal Experience

When you are trying to decide what to write about, a good place to start is your personal experiences. Think through the many life lessons you have learned, trips you have taken, people you have met, hobbies you enjoy, events you have survived, and other parts of your life. What is something you are passionate about? Is it your family? Your job? A favorite pastime?

As you think what to write about, keep your reader in mind. What can someone who reads about your personal experience take away and apply to his or her life? How can you make your personal experiences valuable to those who have not lived them? Occasionally we get so caught up in the personal nature of the experience, we fail to remember there is a reader out there who doesn't care about the experience but is reading and hoping there will be something valuable for him or her. Don't forget the takeaway.

> When you are trying to decide what to write about, a good place to start is your personal experiences.

When the new writer writes a personal experience article, a common mistake is to tell every detail of the experience as well as anything related to that experience. Most of the time you must zero in on one specific experience. Life is full of experiences unrelated but intertwined.

For example, Grace decided she was going to write an article on surviving depression. She started writing and got to the part of her depression journey where she and her husband divorced. *Oh!* She thought. *I need to tell them about my marriage and how it ended in divorce.* Grace continued to write and came to the part where a church member reached out to her and went with her to her counseling and therapy appointments. So, she wrote several hundred words telling how wonderful the fellowship of the church is. The fellowship of the church is important and real. But it is a "rabbit trail" in Grace's article on depression.

Focus on one experience and realize you have several more articles you can write branching off from your original idea of your depression journey.

Calendar Article

Your calendar is a gold mine of ideas and connecting points. A calendar article contains anything related to a season, holiday, anniversary, or other calendar event. You could choose a historical event, a special personal day, or something frivolous that is celebrated nationally such as National Peanut Butter Day.

Many magazines work from a theme list. Before you begin to write you may want to check the guidelines to see if the editorial calendar includes a theme list. Often general themes for magazines include:

> A calendar article contains anything related to a season, holiday, anniversary, or other calendar event.

January – Renewal

February – Relationships

March – Rebirth

April – Stewardship

May—Mother's Day/Memorial Day

June—Father's Day

July –Independence Day

August—Back-to-School

September—Fall

October—Halloween/Columbus Day

November—Thanksgiving

December—Christmas

Avoid the predictable such as What Christmas Means to Me, First Thanksgiving, My Mother—the Best Mother in the World, The Best Advice My Father Ever Gave Me, etc.

For seasonal articles, timing is very important. Be sure to query magazines at least 6-8 months ahead of the season. Check the guidelines to see what their exact lead time is for seasonal articles. When fall is in the air, it is too late to think about pitching Thanksgiving articles. If you need ideas for calendar tie-ins, check the Farmer's Almanac, school days calendars, or online calendars for special days.

Round-Up

A round-up article solicits lots of points of view on the same topic. These types of articles are fun to do and sometimes quicker to complete. Talking to different people about one subject and gathering perspective from a cross-section of people is both interesting and exciting. Then the challenge of bringing all the opinions together in a cohesive article is gratifying.

A round-up article solicits lots of points of view.

Decide on your topic. Then consider who you might contact to give you a paragraph or two on the subject. Choose those who are "experts" either by education or life experience. For an article on the best way to get a toddler to eat his or her vegetables, your demographic would be moms and dads.

Vary the geographic demographic as well. Don't walk around the block and knock on every door in your neighborhood and ask for opinions on a specific subject. Think of people you know from all over the US and contact a few of them from different regions. If appropriate for the magazine, solicit opinions from both males and females.

Put what you are looking for into writing. Be specific and don't assume the person you are approaching can read between the lines. It may help to give them one or two specific questions to answer. If you have written your introduction to the article, include it in the query to potential contributors.

Let them know where you intend to submit the article. If you have already pitched the idea, let contributors know where you have pitched and the status. If you already have a deadline, mention it. If you don't, be sure to state a deadline by which you would like to have their responses. Offer to have a telephone conversation. If they prefer, set up a time and day for that to happen. Be respectful of their time and don't ask for more than you need. For a contribution to a round-up article, fifteen minutes should be plenty.

Choose a topic that is not obscure, and one which will interest readers. Good topics include how to solve a problem or manage a family or business scenario.

Make a list of who you would like to contribute. Some round-up articles could focus on celebrity comments. If you have access to people who are well-known, a celebrity round-up might be fun. Think about Unique Ways to Celebrate on the Road, Special Christmas Memories, The Best Mother's Day Ever, etc. Readers like to read about how famous people celebrate the same holidays and create traditions as they do.

Profile Article

Profile articles are the mainstay of many magazines. Magazines of every kind—religious and secular, local and national, adult and children—are interested in these human-interest articles. Next time you are at a magazine stand, look at the covers. You will see a lot of pictures of individuals. That magazine probably has a feature profile article about the cover person. Their face is on the cover, and there is a story inside.

Profile articles are written in the third person and are the result of interviewing the subject and discovering what is interesting and noteworthy. For a profile article, remember you are looking for a piece of his or her life story, not a generalized overview. A profile article is not a biography. Readers can identify more closely with an in-depth look at one slice of the subject's life than bits and pieces of many years.

> Profile articles are written in the third person and are the result of interviewing the subject and discovering what is interesting and noteworthy.

Before you go for the interview, do your homework. Read as much as you can about the person. If he or she has written books, browse through them so you can be familiar with the highlights of his or her life. If the person is a celebrity, check newspapers for recent articles. If he or she is a businessperson, learn about the business. You don't want to waste valuable interview time asking questions about something you could have already found out through research.

For profile articles, timing is important. A person could be of interest because of a connection to a historical anniversary or calendar day. Perhaps he or she has achieved a much sought-after goal. He or she could have achieved something very few people have. For example, someone who gave birth to 22 biological children all of whom are in the medical profession or someone who climbed to the top of the highest mountain on every continent. Or he or she could be well-known in the entertainment industry. People like to read about other people because they are curious, so profile articles are trendy.

In writing a profile article, be sure to give a complete presentation of the story. If you have done an in-person interview, observe body language. If you have gone to your subject's office or home, observe the surroundings. What are their tastes? Do they collect anything? Are there any family pictures around? All these details are clues to the background and interests of the person you are interviewing.

When setting up the interview, be respectful of the person's time. Decide before you communicate with him or her how much time you need and don't ask for more. When conducting the interview, stay within the requested time frame. If you have not completed your interview, don't stay over unless you are invited to do so. If you need more time, ask if you could do a follow-up phone call with a few more questions or clarifications or if you could meet again for a short time.

Take a recorder or use your phone to record your conversation. The recording helps you get accurate quotes and not leave out any information. Always be sure to ask permission to record your conversation. Most people are very willing for you to record since it ensures the accuracy of their remarks.

If you have trouble finding a contact for someone you want to interview and he or she has written a book, the publisher of the book can probably help you.

Interview Article

The interview article may feel similar to a profile article. And it is, so the information above applies. In most cases, the interview article presents similar information as the profile article in a different way. In fact, you could take the information from your interview you were doing for a profile article and turn it into an interview article if it is a good fit for the magazine.

The interview article can be written in question and answer format. You, the interviewer, ask the question and present the answers from your subject. When written in a magazine, the format is Q & A with the Q being **you** and represented by your initials or the initials of the **magazine and** the A or the initials or name of the interviewed person.

The interview article format allows you to interject narrative between quotes if you desire. So, there is opportunity for you to be somewhat subjective while still preserving much of the conversation with your subject.

Readers also love the Q & A format. They can pick and choose certain aspects of the subject they are only slightly interested in about the person. This type article is also usually a quick read filled with lots of information.

How-To—An Evergreen Form of Article

Evergreen articles present subjects that are always of interest. You may need to update information or change the slant, but the subject never goes out of style. An evergreen article is one people will always be interested in.

How-to articles are always popular because people want to know how to make something, do something, or find a solution for something. They are called evergreen because their subject never grows old.

Evergreen articles keep on selling because the subject matter is always of interest. You can sell evergreen articles to a publication then after a few years refresh the same article with some updated information and sell it again.

There are two types of how-to articles.

1) Tangible How-To

The tangible how-to article tells you how to create something, often using a bulleted list. When you think of tangible how-to articles, recipes may come to mind, how to build something, or how to create a festive centerpiece. When writing a how-to article don't assume the reader knows anything about what you are teaching. If the activity involves cooking, start with basics such as turning on the stove, using the correct size pot, or boiling water.

If the activity involves any tool, make sure you give safety instructions for that tool since the person may not have experience with the tool. When you have written your how-to, be sure to give it a test run. Follow the directions yourself, or better yet, have someone who has never done the topic of the how-to before test it and make sure you achieve the desired results.

> The tangible how-to article tells you how to create something, often using a bulleted list.

Marnie loved to do crafts and decided she would market some of her craft ideas. One of her ideas was a paper mache mask. The day she received an assignment to write a how-to article, she had six children playing at her home for the afternoon. She decided to give her instructions a test run.

"Everyone come here," she called. "I have a fun project for you."

Marnie had covered the kitchen table with paper and had several "stations" for the children. Each station had materials for creating paper-mache masks. Each station had different methods and instructions. What a great test market for the best way to create a mask.

One team used a balloon and put the paper mache directly onto the balloon. Another team crumpled aluminum foil to make a form, leaving room to remove the foil later. The third team used newspaper as their base. All worked diligently and had a great time experimenting with the best way to make a mask.

> The intangible how-to article often contains life lessons you have learned in times of trial or trouble.

"Thank you, children," Marnie said. "You have helped me with my research for this article."

The children were excited about being able to help and even more so when Marnie showed them the article they had helped with. Who says research cannot be fun!

2) Intangible How-To Article

The intangible how-to article often contains life lessons you have learned in times of trial or trouble. These articles lead to self-improvement. Examples of this type article might be How I Overcame Depression, Managing Your Money After Bankruptcy, 10 Ways to Control Your Temper, Taking Care of Loved Ones Who Have Lost Their Minds Without Losing Yours, or Managing My Five-Year-Old.

Intangible how-to articles often follow a specific formula.

Introduction

Depending on your word count, the lead could be a short paragraph with a statistic or question or a longer story about how you came to the point of your solution.

Transition

The transition is the bridge between the opening hook and the helpful information you are going to share with your reader. It doesn't have to be lengthy. Sometimes a sentence will do.

Steps

Here's the how-to part of the article. Even though your introduction is flowing narrative, you need to tell your readers what steps you took to find the solution to your problem. Write the steps in a way easily followed by your readers.

Closure

The conclusion, or wrap up, of your how-to is important. You may want to circle back to your opening and state how your life is different now, pointing out how far you have come. The ending should bring closure as well as encouragement to your readers.

Issue Article

Don't be afraid to write about issues although some writers find this a difficult format. Many issues make national news and international news and are in the forefront of people's minds. Just remember if you are writing an issue article, you must keep it balanced. The temptation is for your opinion to work its way into the article. Present both sides of the issue without bias. Don't get on a soapbox. Keep your opinion separate from the issue article.

If you only present your opinion, then the article becomes an opinion piece and is in a different category.

A hitchhiker article is one that elaborates on or connects in some way to an event in the news. Issue articles often "hitchhike" on the latest news. Today one of the headlines in my newspaper is "City Works to Find Food Truck, Restaurant Balance." When you read that headline, does anything come to mind? Several things might be possibilities for articles that "hitchhike" on this article.

> A hitchhiker article is one that elaborates on or connects in some way to an event in the news.

Are Food Trucks Rated by the Food Inspectors?

Food Trucks—Convenience vs. Dining Experience

Food Trucks—The New Way to Take a Client Out to Lunch

Currently, there are a lot of weather and disaster events happening in the world. Possible article hitchhikers are

How to Be Prepared for a Disaster

Disaster Drills You Should Practice with Your Children

Neighborhood Disaster Preparation

Preparing a Keepsake Box

AUTHOR NOTE

When you have a relationship with an editor, you can email him or her and pitch timely articles to help fill space on days of special events, disasters, or world events. For instance, on the afternoon of September 11, 2001, after talking with my children about what the day's events meant, I wrote what I had said to them. I called it "Talking with Your Children in Times of Disaster." I emailed an editor I worked with frequently, and he invited me to send the article as soon as possible.

Op-Ed Article

Unlike an issue article that must be balanced and give a fair representation of all sides of an issue, an op-ed article is one in which you are free to state your opinion and support it with facts of your choosing. In many newspapers, there is an op-ed page where you see articles of this type as well as letters to the editor which are another way to write an article stating your opinion. This type of article is not always easy to break into because many newspapers have op-ed writers or use syndicated columns.

Devotion

Before you attempt this type of article, differentiate between a devotion and a devotional article.

When we use the word devotion, short 250-350 word articles appearing in devotional magazines or books come to mind. Devotion is the noun and refers to a short, inspirational article sharing part of someone's spiritual journey and encourages and inspires readers to worship and make a spiritual discovery of their own. The word devotional is an adjective and refers to a periodical or book full of devotions. Many denominations produce devotional magazines monthly. You can pick them up at church or subscribe to them. Some of the titles include *Upper Room, Our Daily Bread, The Secret Place, and Open Windows.*

> Devotion refers to a short, inspirational article sharing part of someone's spiritual journey. Devotional refers to a periodical or book full of devotions.

Devotional magazines often give a formula for the writer. Formulaic writing means that the publisher has a specific outline for the writer to follow.

> Formulaic writing means that the publisher has a specific outline for the writer to follow.

Writing for daily devotional magazines is a good place for article writers to break into getting published. The pieces are short and therefore encourage tight writing. Publishers need new material for every day of the year, so there is lots of opportunity. Pay is not usually very high, but these devotions count as a writing credit which is valuable to a writer trying to build a resume.

Several important tips to keep in mind

Your thesis statement should be short—a maximum of 10 words.

Most devotions range from 100-350 words with 250 being the most common.

In the limited word count you have, you must concentrate on one single spiritual point. You do not have enough words to cover more. Focus on a brief, God-centered point drawing the reader's attention to the Lord.

Public domain means that the copyright has expired and no one has legal rights to the material so writers can freely use it without additional permission.

A good way to begin a devotion is a startling fact, a quotation, a small object lesson, short dialogue, or brief anecdote. Just remember not to quote from hymns or poems unless they are in public domain. Public domain means that the copyright has expired and no one has legal rights to the material so writers can freely use it without additional permission. This rule about quotes applies to all article writing.

Some devotions end with a short prayer and/or a thought for the day. The thought for the day should be catchy and stay in the reader's thoughts.

When I wrote my first devotions for a small, non-denominational magazine, I was surprised when I received the format the magazine wanted me to use. Not only was word count specified, but it also said the devotion should contain 21 lines with 38 characters per line. This assignment was in the "old days" when I wrote on a word processor without the benefit of a built-in word or character counter. I was shocked I had to count every character for each line to make sure I was following the instructions perfectly. Working on my first devotion assignment ever, I was excited. But when I saw the amount of work, my excitement waned a bit. It was, however, a good exercise in writing to specific guidelines and has helped me to always check on what is expected when I get an assignment.

A few other tips

If you have the option to use Scripture in the body of the devotion rather than at the beginning, do. Sometimes people read the Scripture and decide the devotion is not for them.

Avoid controversial subjects or talking about death.

Write conversationally as if seated in a coffee shop across the table from a friend.

Do not use phrases like "I think," "I believe." We know you think it or believe it or you wouldn't have written it.

Devotional/Inspirational Article

A devotional article is similar to the devotion described above. The main difference is the length. A devotional article is placed in a magazine or on a website and can be more than 1000 words, about the same length as other articles.

A devotional article takes your inspirational thought and develops it more fully than you can in a short devotion. You still may have one focus thought, but you can develop more points within one thought and use more illustrations. You still want to provide takeaway for the reader and inspire him or her to draw closer to God. Some magazines, websites, and blogs accept longer devotional articles to encourage their readers.

If you are writing for a Christian publication, you can use scripture freely and speak of Jesus, God, and salvation. Your testimony could be part of your illustrations, and you can share how you live out your faith.

An inspirational article should inspire the reader to make a change or meet a challenge in his or her life. After reading the article, readers should want to do better, try something new, or make a change in their attitudes. He or she should finish the article feeling they can accomplish something seemingly unattainable in some way before reading. Inspirational articles are not to be confused with devotional articles and are not necessarily religious.

EXPERT WORD

There is something about longer devotional articles that give the writer a meal instead of a snack.
Beth Patch, Senior Internet Producer, CBN.com

Listicles

One of the new kids on the block (or at least the updated terminology for it) in the world of articles is the listicle. A listicle is an article made up primarily of lists, quotations, charts, or tips centered around a single theme. These items can be numbered or bulleted and usually have additional information to support the items on the list.

> A listicle is an article made up primarily of lists, quotations, charts, or tips centered around a single theme.

Newspapers and magazines welcome listicles for many reasons but especially because of the clear, concise way of communicating information. It is easy to adjust for space simply by deleting one or more of the items on the list. Next time you are at the grocery store or newsstand, browse the magazines on the rack. Do you see one or more listicle? A recent magazine boasts— "3 Ways with Festive Fall Flowers," "10 Brilliant Uses for Petroleum Jelly." Listicles are found in both print and online, but you may find they are more common in blogs and other online writing.

When writing a listicle, you need an introductory paragraph to inform the reader what your article is about. Then you can proceed with your list and any other explanation.

Filler Article

Filler articles are used as their name implies—to fill spaces in the magazine. Often there is a spot at the end of a page too small for an entire article and too large to leave empty. Instead of trying to find another graphic to fill the spot, publishers may insert a joke, fact, very short article, personal experience, news fact, or some other short piece. Not all magazines use fillers so be sure to check the guidelines. Submission format would be the same as a magazine article. Be sure to include word count since that is the best way for publishers to determine if the filler fits their space. Most fillers are short, but occasionally the spot a magazine needs to fill is longer than a few paragraphs.

Children's Article

Writing for children is a great market and a popular market for authors. Some people also have the thought—I'll write for children. It is easier and quicker. That thought is a misconception. Writing for children requires exceptional attention to your target market, meticulous choice of words since you can't use as many, and the writing may not be as easy as you think.

Because the children's market is not the primary one I write for, I asked well-known children's author, Karen Whiting (www.

karenwhiting.com) if she would share a few tips with us about the specifics of children's writing.

1. Children's magazines compete with online fun.

   Grabbing children's attention competes with online fun, so it needs to offer edutainment by layering the writing and weaving in humor. They are used to the Disney WOW and razzle-dazzle online.

2. Articles need to reach a child's abilities and understanding.

3. Know the child's language and reading vocabulary.

4. Do not bore a child, but make reading fun.

   Engage children with humor; make them squirm, surprise them, or intrigue them.

AUTHOR NOTE

The other day I told my granddaughter to read her school book before she began playing. "Do I have to read at the table?" she asked.

"No," I said, "as long as you get your reading done, it doesn't matter where you read."

Moments later I looked out the window. My grandson had talked Grandpa into letting him drive the utility vehicle around the farm. He smiled as he drove for what couldn't have been more than two miles an hour. In the back of the vehicle was my granddaughter, relaxing and reading her school book!

---

5. Help children feel and care about others (they do not naturally have compassion or understand what someone else is going through).

   Connect emotionally by using truth, fresh perspectives, and examples.

Use engaging characters and new ideas to illuminate minds (not sanitized views) and motivate kids to be world changers and to care about the needs of other people.

They want to be empowered to help others, so share a few starter ideas.

They want to build relationships, and so they need to understand other people.

6. Build in word clues because children are learning and not all know the same words, but it frustrates them not to understand what they are reading.

When using unfamiliar words, provide context clues.

Examples:
- The speaker received a small stipend, or payment, for her talk.
- The leader said, "Climbing the mountain is grueling. You'll be very tired when we reach the top."

7. Tap into Senses
- Sight sets the scene: tire swing in yard, old door creaked, spiky hair
- Noise (hearing) lays a soundtrack: giggle, chortle, growl, wheel screeched
- Scents evoke memories (chicken pot pie, smelly socks, sour milk, rain in the air)
- Touch evokes emotions (feelings of pain, pleasure) pricked his finger, kitten's rough tongue licked his cheek, he slid on the wet, slippery, rocks
- Taste taps into hunger, thirst, memories: munched the crunchy chips, licked the vanilla ice cream, tasted the salty ocean breeze

8. Children's periodicals often use theme lists, so check and see if the one you want to write for does and then submit for the appropriate theme.

9. The easiest way to break in is usually with games and puzzles. Determine what the theme of the magazine is and create a word search or rebus to go along with the theme.

10. Read the letters to the editor and children's comments to get ideas of what they like.

11. Know the age level you are writing for and differences on how to write for them.
    Young children enjoy onomatopoeia.
    Children like the main character to be a little older than their age.
    Tweens are at the crossroads between concrete thinking and abstract, critical thinking. They want help navigating their world, but it must sound real to them.

EXPERT WORD

Writing for children requires some mathematics. Have no fear though, writers, because the equation is simple addition and subtraction. You'll add in the identical skills you've learned through writing adult articles. Then subtract unnecessary words, and finish the article with a kid-friendly bottom line.
Terri Kelly, Author of *Mary Slessor: Missionary Mother*,
www.terribkelly.com

Book Reviews

Have you read a good book lately? Do you have an opinion about the book?

Perhaps you could write book reviews. When you have read the book, you have done your research. Now write your thoughts on the book itself and what group of people might be interested in it.

A book review is not a summary or a book report. It is tempting to write a summary similar to the book reports you used to write in school. But you only need to give your readers enough information to know what the book is about. Then you can give them additional pieces as examples of your opinion.

Was their controversy in the book? Did it cause you to think or rethink your position on a subject? Was there a challenge for the reader?

Many publishers have a list of reviewers to send books to when they are released.

EXPERT WORD

As an avid reader, I love to share my thoughts and opinions about books. And I enjoy promoting the works of others. So, book reviews is a good fit for me.

Like all good writing, book reviews need to open with a hook. My blog, "Reading Between the Lines," looks for spiritual applications that are not obvious.

An effective book review averages between 300 and 500 words. Writing book reviews helped me learn to write tighter and get the point across in fewer words.

Gerry Wakeland, blogger of "Reading Between the Lines."

Columns

A column is a series of articles strung together because they are on the same subject. Columns are a regular feature of many magazines and websites and provide writers with a way to have a steady gig. Some writers gather their columns and put them together in a book.

If you are interested in pitching a column to a magazine, study existing columns. Find a new subject area you could write about, find a magazine interested in your topic but without a column, and pitch. Submit three to six columns with your pitch so the editor can see how you would handle the topic.

A column is a series of articles strung together because they are on the same subject.

EXPERT WORD

I have been a columnist for more than 40 years in both newspapers and magazines and, more recently, via a weekly blog. Whereas it is true writing a column can provide a form of steady income and continuous name recognition and national visibility, of greater value to me is the pressure a column puts on me. When I know I have a weekly or monthly deadline to produce copy that will entertain, teach, and encourage my readers, it motivates me to read voraciously, to engage in conversations with fascinating people, and to stay current with movies, TV shows, politics, science, religion, and art. I can only earn the trust and loyalty of my readers if I continue to produce stimulating and insightful columns. That requires having the five senses on full alert for understanding contemporary topics, issues, and events.

Dennis E. Hensley, Ph.D.
Finding Success with Your Dream Writing Projects

Chapter 8
Elements of Articles

When you have your idea in place, consult the guidelines of the magazine to ensure you can provide all the elements they request. Many are very similar, but if a periodical has unusual specifics, the guidelines include them. Some things to consider are listed below.

Length—There is no standard length. The guidelines provide a range of the number of words. Magazines have a reason for restricting word count. Only so many words fit on a page, usually around 600 words for one page depending on how many and how large the graphics. They much prefer to be able to print the entire article on one page unless there is enough to fill two. Two pages hold around 1100-1200 words and create a spread. They also need room for art, photos, and other graphic elements. So, follow the guidelines since each magazine knows best what works for their publication.

Articles come in all sizes. Teaching articles can often be a little longer than the usual narrative article.

A word here about article length. Many new writers ask the question—How do I know how long my article is going to be? Most of the time when you have an idea for an article, you also know one or more publications that might be interested. Read the guidelines for those magazines and then let the average number of words be your target. You can adjust if needed when you decide exactly where to submit your article. Since you have just begun to develop your idea, write to their specifications instead of writing blindly with no target figure in mind then having to cut words later.

Title—Keep your title brief and appropriate. Remember the title is the first thing the editor reads when you submit the article and the first thing your reader sees. Readers may even decide as to whether to read the rest of the article based on the title. Work hard to create a title demanding attention. Keeping your title as short as possible is a good idea. If you need more words to express your idea, many magazines use subtitles. Studying two or three issues of the magazine will give you an idea of title length and whether to use a subtitle. Titles cannot be copyrighted so even if another article or book has the same title, it is not a problem. However, if a title is overused, you may want to think of a new one for your article so yours won't get lost in the pile!

Hook/Lead—This is the first paragraph of your article. The reason it is called the hook is its purpose is to "hook" the reader and draw him or her into the article. Another word for the hook is the lead. Another good word. The purpose of the "lead" is to lead the reader right into the rest of the article. Make him or her care about what you say. No matter what you call it, the first paragraph or paragraphs should pull the reader into the rest of the article and invite him or her to read on.

There are several types of hooks or leads. Most of them fall into one of the following categories.

- Narrative—The narrative lead opens your article with a story. The writer may use an anecdote, dialogue, or a hypothetical vignette.

- Descriptive—The descriptive lead paints a visual picture setting the story.

- Question—The question lead makes the reader begin to think right away. Hopefully, it draws him or her in and make him curious enough to read on.

- Quotation—Using a quotation from someone other than the author brings credibility to the table right from the beginning. Quotes could be from a famous person, a literary work, or a play or movie.

- Thematic—The thematic lead introduces the reader to the point of the article. This lead could include a statement about the problem the article addresses.

- Point—This is the "meat" of the article. The meat, or point, of the article is the main idea you are communicating with your readers. You develop the point in many ways, and it lets the reader know exactly what you want him or her to learn and take away from their reading.

- Support—The support of your article are the embellishments that flesh out your point. The support may include colorful anecdotes, Scripture, illustrations, statistics—anything illustrating your point and helping your readers understand what your article is about. If appropriate, include personal experiences to let the reader get to know you. Readers will identify with writers who are open and honest about their lives. As readers get to know you, they realize your writing has truthful, viable answers to the subject at hand.

- Dialogue—Often writers think they must reserve dialogue for fiction where conversations abound. However, dialogue is very useful with nonfiction as well. Inserting a conversation between two people on the subject of your article makes it personal to the reader and helps him or her feel as if he or she is eavesdropping on part of the conversation.

When you begin to write, you often hear instructors say, "Show, don't tell." Dialogue is helpful when it comes to showing.

If your article was called "The Art of Conversation" and one paragraph read:

> When you meet a new friend, it is often helpful to engage him or her in conversation about something familiar. Perhaps the person lives in your neighborhood or your children go to school together. When you have established common ground, you can then talk about other areas. Be sensitive to the demeanor of your new friend. If a subject seems uncomfortable, don't go there.

Save that conversation for another time. Make sure you are personable and welcoming to your friend and even your body language is positive.

Instead of writing it that way you might say:

At the meeting, Mary noticed a couple she didn't know. They stood at the edge of the room, silent, arms folded. Mary crossed the room and extended her hand. "Hi," Mary said. "I haven't seen you at our neighborhood meetings before. Have you just moved in?"

"Yes, my name is Sheila. And this is my husband, Drew. Are these meetings always this well attended?"

"Sheila, I'm Mary. Hello, Drew. And, yes, they are. This neighborhood is wonderful to live in. There are lots of children. Do you have children?"

Sheila shifted feet, and her eyes stayed on the floor. "Yes."

Mary sensed Sheila didn't want to talk about her family right then. She took a step closer to Sheila, reached out and gently put her hand on her elbow, and said, "Let me introduce you to some of the other ladies. Drew, let me find my husband, and you and he can meet some of the great guys around here. Come this way."

Aha! — This is the moment when the article becomes important to the reader. He or she has grasped the point and sees there is an exciting takeaway in store. Your reader begins to understand why you thought this was important enough to write about and why it is important to him or her. You have inspired him or her to internalize the understanding and make an effort to apply some of the principles in your article.

Wrap—In the wrap portion of your article you are summarizing so your reader is satisfied with the outcome. As you bring the article to a close, the reader begins to reflect on the information he or she has absorbed. Your wrap may include a challenge to your reader or an action step related to your article.

There are several effective ways to end an article.

- Your article could end with a call to action for the reader.

- You could circle back to the lead and reinforce or continue a thought introduced there.

- Just as a thought-provoking question can be a good way to begin an article, it can also be a good way to end. You leave your reader with something to think about.

- A summary of the article and the importance of its main points is good reinforcement.

- Quotations can also be a good ending and add additional meaning to your article.

- A shocking statement is a good way to bring the article to a close and wake the reader to the importance of its message.

- Close with a new anecdote or the continuation of the one you used as the lead.

Stop when your article is done. Some writers have difficulty stopping. Don't be one of them. When you have said all that needs to be said, don't keep writing. A benefit to the reader of shorter articles is they are easier to remember.

Whatever method you choose, make the ending memorable.

Several ways you can add features to your article to make it more attractive to editors and publishers are simple and carry out the theme of your article.

Sidebars—Sidebars are the separate boxes that give additional information about the subject of the article. Sometimes

Sidebars are the separate boxes that give additional information about the subject of the article.

the information is in bulleted format. Sometimes it is a mini article. Or it could be a personal experience testimony of someone who can make your writing more meaningful.

For example, you are writing an article on depression. This article is a personal experience telling about your journey through depression and how you overcame it. You have drawn the reader in, and he or she is tracking with you. About halfway through, you begin telling about one of the people who helped identify your illness and get you help. The thought pops into your head you should tell people what to look for in others who may be depressed. Should you stop in the middle of your personal experience and state all the warning signs of depression?

No! This is where your sidebar becomes important. Instead of interrupting the flow of your article, put the information in a sidebar. In other words, your article is titled "My Journey Through Depression." Your sidebar will be "10 Warning Signs of Depression." By using the additional information in a sidebar, you have given the reader useful information, and yet it was not intrusive to your story. Additionally, graphic designers love sidebars because they become a graphic element on the page. Your sidebar becomes like a piece of art and adds interest to the page.

The reverse to the above scenario can be true. You could write an informative article about depression, its warning signs, and treatments and your sidebar could be a personal experience of someone who had struggled to overcome depression.

When submitting your manuscript, start the sidebar on a new page and treat it just as you did your article listing word count and other information. Sidebars can be bulleted or numbered lists, how-to, or just a short narrative that had no place in the main article. Occasionally a sidebar could be a testimony piece or personal experience of someone who has experienced the topic of the article or is an expert in that field. Sidebars are usually short, although they could run any length at the editor's discretion.

A hot box only has room for one or two lines.

When you pitch an article with a related sidebar, one thing you need to remember is you are pitching two items that go together but are not inseparable. In other words, even though you are pitching two items you think are a package, the editor can decide to buy one or the other or both.

Another feature you can add to your article is a "hot box." This feature is similar to a sidebar but smaller. A hot box only has room for one or two lines. Along with our article on "My Journey Through Depression," we might offer a hot box with the national help line for those suffering from depression. This small box with one piece of useful information could be a lifeline to others.

Callouts are also effective as an additional feature with an article. In fact, some editors request a callout for every so many words. A callout is words you see on the page that are bigger than the article type that calls attention to that thought.

A callout is words you see on the page that are bigger than the article type that calls attention to that thought.

A callout usually comes from a sentence in the text. Some editors still refer to callouts as pull quotes.

Author Bios

Almost without exception, you will be asked for an author bio when you submit an article for publication. A bio is also called a bio sketch. Bios give the editor, reader, and publisher information about you, your background, and your qualifications to write on your subject. Be sure to send the publication the type of bio they are looking for. Check the guidelines which may tell you by word count how much space there is for the bio. Remember to write tightly so you can get as much information as possible into the few words you are allocated. If the bio is not mentioned, look at a copy of the publication. Go to the bottom of the articles and see what type bios they use and similarly structure your bio.

The author bio should be written in third person. Don't be shy. Take advantage of your chance to brag about yourself a bit and highlight accomplishments pertinent to the publication you are writing for. Be sure to include your website.

Bios give the editor, reader, and publisher information about you, your background, and your qualifications to write on your subject.

Make your bio interesting. Just because it is factual information about you doesn't mean your bio should put your reader to sleep. Make it humorous if possible. Or interject a little known interesting fact about yourself. Making your bio memorable ensures your reader remembers as well.

You may want to keep several versions of your bio in your computer, so, when you need a bio of a certain length, it is readily available. Keeping bios updated makes it easy to quickly access current information.

Have a long version of your bio listing education, work experience, writing credits, volunteer experience, and organizations you belong to. Edit it a bit to a smaller size you can customize to send with article submissions. Then create a shorter bio note for smaller writing projects. When possible, tie your bio into the article you are writing.

For instance, if you write an article on "Taking Care of the Family Dog," you might end your bio like this. Linda's family includes her husband, children, grandchildren, and Gregory and Charlotte, their family boxers.

There are several types of bios, most based on the number of words you can use.

Full Bio—The full bio is your longer version, such as a resume. List complete information about your training, education, work experience, writing credits, volunteer experience, organizations, and family. You use this bio on your website, book proposals, interviews, speaker introductions, and media kits. You can find a copy of the author's long bio at the end of this book.

Shorter Bio—This bio is probably less than 100 words and includes brief information about your qualifications and a specific tie-in to the article you are writing. For example, if you are writing an article about how to make the best cherry pie ever, you would want to include in your bio that your cherry pie won first place for three years in a row at the county fair. If you were writing an article on best ways to discipline your toddler, the fact that you raised eight children would be important. Similarly, if you are writing about the secret lives of FBI agents, it would be important to know you were an agent before your retirement. You would use this version when you write a query for an article or shorter marketing materials.

Example: Linda Gilden is an award-winning author, speaker, editor, ghostwriter, and writing coach. Author of eleven books and over a thousand magazine articles, Linda loves helping others discover the joy of writing. As a member of the CLASSeminars training staff and director of two writers conferences, Linda takes writers to the next step in their writing journeys. Her most recent book is *Words to Live By*. Linda lives in SC with family and especially loves every minute spent with her six grandchildren. She is currently working on a series, Camp Grandma, that includes many of their adventures. Visit www.lindagilden.com.

Bio Note—A bio note is just that. A short note saying all about you in a sentence or two, usually 50 words or less. This type of bio is probably the least used, but some magazines use it in your byline or you can use it for social media.

Example: Linda Gilden is an award-winning writer and speaker who loves living on the farm where the entire family visits often. Learn more at www.lindagilden.com.

Professional Author Photo

You do not need a photo for every article you write. When you do need one, make sure you have the very best likeness you can get. This is part of your marketing identity. Use the same photo on all your articles, book covers, social media, and business cards. Anywhere you use a photo use the best one you have. People begin to see the photo and immediately think of you without having to study the photo to see if it is someone they know.

Make sure you update your photo as needed. Some people look the same for years while others look differently every time you see them.

Hire a professional. It is worth the investment to have photos taken by a professional photographer. He or she has been trained in the best use of the equipment as well as how to use lighting, backgrounds, and setting to make you look your best. You will use your photo not only with article bios and book covers but also on social media where it can reach hundreds of thousands. This picture is put out there to the world so you want it to be the best it can be. However, do not have it touched up so much it no longer looks like you!

AUTHOR NOTE

A nationally known author and speaker came to my church to conduct a conference. She was staying with one of our church ladies who waited until the evening with her son for our guest to arrive. The hostess decided since it was so late she would get ready for bed and left her 12-year-old son listening for the doorbell. Along with a reminder to be polite and welcome her, she gave her son a brochure with the author's picture on it so he would recognize her when she rang the doorbell.

The hostess went upstairs. Not too long after, the doorbell rang. The son checked the brochure, welcomed the guest, and showed her to her room.

He went upstairs to tell his mom their guest had arrived. Knock, knock. "Mom."

"Yes, son. Is she here?"

"Well," her son said a little hesitantly.

"Is something wrong?"

"No, nothing is wrong." Pause. "But I think she sent her mother."

Good reason to update your picture. You sure don't want anyone to think your mother wrote your article!

Below is a sample first page of a manuscript mailed to a periodical. Type your name and personal and contact information at the top of the page, single-spaced.

Name   Rights You Are Offering
Address   About ??? Words
City and Zip
Email address
Phone
Website

Title
The title should be one-third of the way down the page.

By Pen Name
(If you are not using a pen name, do not include this
line. The editor will know your name because it is
listed above. Only use this line to establish the article
will be written under a pen name.)

The appearance of your manuscript is important. Start with good quality white paper. Don't use unusual fonts, stickers, or confetti to make your page look cute. Editors don't like that! Choose an easily read font such as Times New Roman. Double-space your copy and leave one to one-and-a-half-inch margins all the way around. The extra space allows room for proofing marks. Don't justify your right margin, just the left one. Only use one space after a period. (Very important! Many argue that they learned in typing class to use two spaces. But you are no longer in typing class! This is the publishing world, and you don't want to mark yourself as a newbie by clinging to the two-space rule.)

Put your last name, a few words of your title, and the page number at the top of the page. This is called a "slug line." Start using the slug line on the second page. The "slug line" consists of a few words of your title, your last name, and the page number. Start numbering on page two. Paper clip the pages together, never staple.

Make sure you spell-check. Then reread to make sure spell-check has not missed something. Sometimes homophones are missed by your computer spell checker. A homophone sounds like another word but is spelled differently—won, one; their, they're, there; two, too, to, and so on. Read your manuscript aloud to check for flow and ease of reading.

Your manuscript may be on the editor's desk with many other submissions. Make your work stand out by using good form and submitting a crisp, clean, well-written copy. Recheck guidelines to make sure you have followed them exactly.

Chapter 9
Payment and Rights to Sell

Another question new writers ask is "How much money am I going to get paid for writing an article?"

Every magazine has a unique pay scale, so there is no one answer to that question. Payment can range from $0 to $1 or $2 per word. Most paying markets, especially for beginning writers, are somewhere in the middle. As you gain more experience, you will write for higher paying markets. Some magazines have a sliding scale where your first articles written for them are for a nominal fee and as you write more, your payment increases.

Clips are copies of published magazine articles you have written.

Market guides list the average pay per article to give you an idea. Your contract or email agreement establishes an agreed-upon amount for your work and when you will be paid. Occasionally you and a publisher agree for you to write an article for a set amount and for some reason the article is never published. In that case, you may be due a kill fee. A kill fee is a fee that is paid when

A kill fee is a fee that is paid when a contracted article is never published.

a contracted article is never published. Kill fees are not the total amount you are promised but a percentage of the original fee. Many times, it is about 50% of the amount. If you are paid a kill fee, you are free to market the article to other publications as a new article since it was never published.

Another frequent question is "Should I ever write for free?" There are varying opinions about that question. Many writers write at least a few things for free when they are getting started. This is a good way to build your portfolio and have some "clips" to show possible editors. Clips are copies of published magazine articles you have written. Often when working with a new writer, an editor asks to see clips of his or her work. With all the online editions of magazines, e-zines, and blogs, it is now possible to send links to your work rather than having to print and mail copies. Writing for free also helps you get your name established in a certain field of writing.

When you sell an article to a publisher, you are selling them the rights to publish your article. You are not selling the article, but the rights to publish those words in that arrangement under whatever agreement you have come to. Rights are a complicated subject and one which you must understand to operate successfully and generate the most income from your writing in the publishing world. As shown on our manuscript submission sample earlier, you must state what

A compilation book is a collection of articles/stories, usually on a single theme.

rights you are offering when you submit your manuscript. There are several choices.

When your article is accepted, your contract again lists the rights you are selling. Check carefully and make sure the magazine is offering to purchase the same rights you are offering.

Sometimes you may offer first rights, but all a magazine is interested in is all rights. That's an important reason to read the guidelines and make sure the rights you want to sell are the same ones the magazine, compilation book, blog, e-zine, or other buys. Most publications state in their guidelines what rights they buy. If, upon examining your contract you don't want to sell the type of rights they purchase, ask if they would consider first rights or one time rights.

All Rights

A few magazines and compilation books still buy all rights. But this is one type of rights you may not want to sell. The publisher buys complete rights to your material, and you have no further claim to it. To sell all rights means you have sold your story to the publisher, who can then publish it as many times as he likes in any form (print, digital, or other) and he doesn't have to pay you any more money. He owns the rights to it.

Keep in mind, however, what you have sold is your story told with that arrangement of words only. You are not selling your story, only that specific version of your story. You are free to rewrite it with different words and sell it again, use it in a book, or whatever you like. Just remember you can't just change a few words around. The entire article must be written with an almost completely new arrangement and choice of words.

If you want to sell your story again, use new anecdotes, a brand new better-than-ever lead, and updated or new statistics. The way to rewrite the story is to sit down and write it without looking at the one you sold all the rights to. When you finish, you can read them both to see if you left anything out. You may find you have grown as a writer, and the second version is even better than the first!

You may be wondering why anyone would ever want to sell all rights. There are several reasons you might consider selling all rights. If the magazine is extremely high profile and you really would like to have a credit on your resume from that magazine, you may consider selling them all rights since you receive an excellent credit on your resume. If it is a story you may never tell again, all rights may not be such a bad thing. Sometimes compilation books (A compilation book is a collection of articles/stories, usually on a single theme.) and devotional magazines buy all rights. The payment for all rights is usually higher than first rights and may be another reason to consider selling all rights.

Work for Hire

Work for Hire is similar to selling all rights. The difference is if you contract for work for hire, you have no rights to the material and no copyright connection. You are working for someone else, and the material is the product of that employer. The copyright is in the name of the person who hired you to do the work. You can never use the material again or offer it to another publication.

One of the biggest differences between all rights and work for hire is that when you sell all rights, the rights eventually, after 35 years, revert to you and you can once **again market the** piece. Work for hire never reverts to the author because it never belonged to the author in the first place.

Many times, work for hire is done by a staff person of the business or publishing house contracting the work. But more and more, freelancers are getting jobs once staff-written because businesses are downsizing and staffs are smaller.

A noncompeting publication is one whose audience is not the same as the original publication.

First Rights

First rights is a term that pretty well explains itself. You are offering the right to publish your article for the first time only—and only in that publication. The publisher has the rights to the article only for the period of initial publication. After a certain period, the rights revert to the author, and you are free to sell it again as a reprint. Check your contract to find out what time period you have to wait until you can offer the article to someone else. For some it is 30 days, some 60, and others 90. It should be stated precisely in the contract.

Remember, you can only offer first rights on an article one time, and not first rights to many publications. First rights refers to rights for the life of an article. When an article has been printed, it can no longer be offered as a first-rights piece.

First North American Serial Rights

First North American Serial Rights, sometimes called FNASR, refers to the first time your article is published in North America. Rights for other countries are also available. The word serial in the title of these rights denotes you are offering it to a periodical. At first glance, you may think you are offering some series to the publication. But the word serial also refers to periodicals. If you are writing in the United States, FNASR is the same thing as first rights.

One Time Rights

Although this may seem similar to first rights it is not the same thing. One time rights gives the publisher license to publish your work one time, but it may not be the first time it was published. One time rights is similar to reprint rights since you are offering material already in print or on the web.

Reprint Rights or Second Rights

Reprints, also referred to as second rights, are a great way to make a little more money without doing a lot of additional work. When your article has been published, and the waiting period, if any, has passed, you can market your article to other publications. You can send it out as a reprint to as many noncompeting publications as you like. A noncompeting publication is one whose audience is not the same as the original publication.

For example, if you have an article printed in *HomeLife*, which is the Baptist family publication, you can offer it as a reprint to *The Lutheran, The Pentecostal Evangel, Light and Life*, and other denominational publications. Baptists rarely read Methodist publications, Lutherans don't read the Pentecostal periodicals, etc.

Same thing would work with parenting articles. If you have placed an article in the magazine and once it is in print you decide to offer it as a reprint, look for noncompeting markets. *Atlanta Parent*, the *Michiana Family Magazine*, and the *Northeast Ohio Parent Magazine* probably do not share the same audience.

With the explosion of the web market, many sites just "borrow" content from other sites and, unfortunately, often get away with that practice. For that reason, it is a good idea to enter your name in a Google alert so you know when it pops up online.

If you don't know how to do this, it is very simple. Go to http://www.google.com/alerts/ then follow the simple directions. In the box asking what you would like the alert to be, type your name. You can also use this service to follow certain subjects you are writing about. Or put your new book title in the box to see where it has been mentioned. Google alerts can be a time saver for your research as well as helping you keep track of where your material is published.

Here is a sample response from Orlando freelance writer Lisa Kaminski Beach (www.LisaBeachwrites.com) when she found her work on a website that had not contacted her to request permission.

Dear (Editor's Name),

I was surprised to find my reprint titled ("Reprint Title") published in the (date) issue of (Magazine/Website Name). I did not realize you were interested in publishing this piece or that it was already published.

While I always enjoy being published, I'd appreciate if you contact me before running my pieces to let me know of your intent. However, since you've already published the piece, I'm now sending you the attached invoice. My reprint fee for this piece is $X.

I'm also attaching my reprint list if you're interested in future articles on parenting and (insert any other topics you cover). Please contact me if you'd like to review any of these pieces and, as a professional courtesy, give me a heads-up if and when you plan to publish any of them. Thank you.

Sincerely,
(Your Name)

This letter professionally states what the author needs to know as well as alerting the website to the fact she is aware they have used her article without permission. By offering other articles for publication with them, the author gives them the opportunity to purchase additional articles thereby keeping her foot in the door with that magazine or website.

When do the rights revert to me? That question will most likely be answered in your contract. Check carefully before signing to make sure the publisher is offering to buy the same thing you are offering. Misunderstandings are much more easily cleared up early in the process rather than later. Some of the options as to when the article rights revert to you maybe as soon as it is in print, 30 days, 60 days, or whatever period the publisher chooses.

Making sure you understand your rights not only eliminates misunderstanding but also allows your mind to think of the next steps for your article creatively.

Electronic Rights

Electronic rights refer to the right to publish your work online or in any digital mode. When websites first became popular, electronic rights were a separate item on article contracts and you could either sell them or not. Now electronic rights are part of what the publisher is buying when he or she purchases your article. These days magazines publish the print version of the magazine then post most articles on their websites.

Chapter 10
Copyright

Writers, especially new writers, have many questions about copyright. Some of those include:

- What do I need to do to protect my work?
- Will someone steal my idea before I get it copyrighted?
- How can I copyright my work?
- What is the length of time between copyrighting and protection?
- Are plagiarism and copyright infringement the same thing?

The answer to some of those questions is found in a straightforward explanation of copyright. When you have written or typed your words on the paper, you own the copyright. It's as simple as that. If you want to register your unpublished work with the United States Copyright Office, you may do so for a fee. The only time that would be of benefit is if a dispute arose concerning the ownership of the material and you had to prove in court who is the owner of the material.

> When you have written or typed your words on the paper, you own the copyright.

If you are going to use your work as a handout when teaching a class or for critique in a writers group, put the word copyright or the copyright sign (©) and your name. If you are submitting it to a publisher, you do not need to worry about including the copyright symbol. Those in the publishing business are aware of the rule and know you own the copyright.

The issue of copyright is important to writers. They want to make sure no one "steals" their material, and they retain the right to use their words wherever they wish with their writing. New writers are often overly concerned about someone stealing their work and not paying them for it.

Are ideas taken from one person and written into article form by another? Occasionally. But as team members in the publishing profession, we must trust each other. Because if we don't risk submitting our ideas and manuscripts to a publisher or editor, our writing can never make a difference for readers because they will never see it in print.

The moment you create a document, whether handwritten or typed into your computer, you own the copyright to that material. It is that simple. Some folks want to complicate the copyright issue, but it all comes down to the fact that if you wrote it, you own it.

If you want to register your idea with the Copyright Office at the Library of Congress in Washington, D.C., forms can be found at www.copyright.gov/forms. There is a charge for this service. Even though their material is protected because it is written, some people prefer to have their work registered with the Copyright Office. A lot of paperwork is involved, and it can get quite expensive if you register every piece of your writing.

> Plagiarism occurs when someone copies the words of someone else and puts his or her name on the document as the author.

A Word about Plagiarism

Writers often confuse plagiarism and copyright infringement. And while there

130

are similarities, one can occur without the other. As writers, we must take be careful not to commit either.

Plagiarism occurs when someone copies the words of someone else and puts his or her name on the document as the author. This "stealing" of words is not legal or ethical and could occur if someone copied a blog post because they liked what it said and posted it on their blog without giving attribution to the author, leaving the readers to think it was an original post.

Copyright infringement occurs when someone copies the words of another complete with attribution but does not have permission to copy or distribute the work.

Copyright infringement occurs when someone copies the words of another complete with attribution but does not have permission to copy or distribute the work. An example of how this could happen would be if a choral group copies music and lyrics for practice and does not have permission to make copies of the work. The author's name remains on the piece, but permission to distribute is lacking.

Copyright allows writers to protect their intellectual property thereby being free to use their work in whatever manner they choose without fear of infringement.

Keep in mind ideas cannot be copyrighted. Titles cannot be copyrighted either. So, when you speak of the copyrighting of material you have written, you are only talking about owning the copyright to the exact arrangement of words that tells your story.

AUTHOR NOTE

When I first started writing, I also feared someone might take my work. I mailed my work to myself. I was told as long as it remained unopened, it was proof of the creation date and copyright ownership. However, many years later I found one of those envelopes and thought to myself—What in the world could this be? Curious, I opened it, thus nullifying any proof of the creation date. These days, you can accomplish the same thing by emailing your manuscript to yourself when it is done. The email would always have the date on it and remain in your mailbox. I'm not sure if this would hold up in a court situation but for the time my envelope was unopened on my shelf, it gave me peace of mind.

Chapter 11
Marketing Your Articles

Unless you match your article with the correct publication, blog, website, or other media form, you will not be able to make a sale.

The first step is to know exactly to whom you are writing. Target your market, know your audience, or research specifically your reader group.

Here's an excellent visual illustration. Think of going out to the archery range and getting out your bow, loading the arrow, lifting it up, and then realizing you were going to just shoot randomly in front of you. Would your result be a successful hit of your target? Of course not, because you had no clue what you were trying to hit. Every good archer knows to hit a bull's eye you have to aim very carefully.

The same principle applies in writing when you begin to market your articles. Before you add words to your article, you need to have a visual in your mind of the reader. That leads to also having an idea of what magazines that reader reads.

It is a good idea when you are preparing to write your article to make a list of possible publications. Read their guidelines. Know their target audience. When you realize several that are a good fit for your material, you are ready to begin to craft your article to reach their readers. Some writers find a picture in a magazine of a person who looks like their vision of their target reader and post it above their computer. Give your reader a name. Some writers even create a personality profile and characteristics list. Then it is easy to communicate with your reader in a way he or she understands. Your target audience becomes real as you welcome the face of the reader into your office and writing realm.

EXPERT WORD

At the Mount Hermon Christian Writers Conference, bestselling author Jerry B. Jenkins spoke of his experience years before, representing Moody Monthly.

"People would ask if I'd be interested in an article about a topic," Jenkins said. "I'd say I'm not interested in an article about something, but an article for the purpose of something."

In other words, what it aims to accomplish in the life of a reader.

That's an aspect few consider as they write and as they query an editor. It's never about you; it's about the reader—and what your writing will do for them.

Remember that, and editors will come to remember you.

Andy Scheer, Andy Scheer Editorial Services
(www.andyscheer.com)

The next step as you begin to write is to consider where to submit. Studying the markets is the best way to become familiar with magazines, e-zines, blogs, and websites looking for material.

How do you study the markets?

First, look at the periodicals you read regularly. Why do they appeal to you? Have you ever read an article and when you finished you said to yourself, "I could have written that!" Or maybe, "I could do better." If you read a magazine regularly, you are probably already familiar with the types of articles it publishes, who the advertisers are (which gives you a clue who the readers are), and the format and style of the writing. Use that information to your advantage. Perhaps one of these magazines would be a logical place for you to start your journey to publication by submitting an article.

If you want to peruse the many magazines on the market, take a trip to your local library. Find a spot near the periodicals and camp out there for a while. You can spend as much time as you like. You can discover new markets similar to the ones you like that might be new possibilities for your writing. Most publishers are glad to send sample copies to prospective writers as well. There may be a small charge, or you may have to pay for postage, but it is worth it. Today, most magazines have a website where they publish the same material as is in the print version, often adding a few more articles. You can look at those on the magazine's website and decide if you could submit articles for the web version of the publication.

The short phrases across the front of the magazine are called cover lines.

You can learn a lot from the magazines you read every day. Look at the cover. The short phrases across the front of the magazine are called cover lines. They give you a clue about what is inside the magazine. Many subjects dot the covers mixed in with pictures of people, food, decorator items, and the like. Health, finance, relationships, self-help to name a few. You can also tell a lot from the cover picture. If it is a person, you can assume the magazine uses profile articles inside. If there is a picture of a decorated room,

The masthead is the box on one of the first pages that has the editors and staff names listed.

then home improvement and decorating are some of the subjects probably covered. Pictures of food? Then perhaps they have a section devoted to recipes or meal preparation.

Opening the magazine, you come to the table of contents and the masthead. The masthead is the box on one of the first pages that has the editors and staff names listed. Sometimes you also find information such as website, corporate address, mission statement, and submission details. Is the masthead large or small? The size of the masthead lets you know the size of the staff and the amount of opportunity for freelance writers.

Compare the writers' names you find in the table of contents with the names in the masthead. If there are a lot of matches, you can surmise many of the articles are staff-written. It is not unusual for an editor to assign one of his or her staff an article to write. However, in most magazines, even though there are a lot of masthead names in the table of contents, there are probably others not there. This means those articles are written by freelancers, and the magazine could be open to your submissions.

Look at the subjects in the table of contents. Are they compatible with the subjects you want to write? Are there regular departments also accepting articles? Or are the departments written by regular columnists? Is there a column idea you have that could fill a gap? Read a few and see if you could fit in with the theme of the department. Often these theme-specific shorter sections are easier to break into.

As you begin your journey through the magazine, take note of the advertisements. Who are they targeting? What age group? What gender? What is the educational level target? What socio-economic group? Who would be likely to purchase the advertised items?

Look at the articles.

- Do they have subtitles as well as titles?
- What is the length of the articles?
- What is their tone? Are they chatty, scholarly, or educational?
- How do they begin? Do they use anecdotes, quotations, controversial statements, or statistics?

- Do the leads make you want to keep reading?

- Are they written in first person? Third person?

- Do they use quotes from experts? If so, how are they attributed? How many quotes do they use?

- Do they use sidebars?

- How frequently is the magazine published? The frequency of publication affects the number of articles needed.

- Are there any shorter articles or fillers?

AUTHOR NOTE

When I wrote my first article for *Writer's Digest*, I found an article similar to the one I was pitching. I opened the magazine next to my computer and item by item observed their formatting preferences. For instance, there was a title, so I created one of about the same length. There was a subtitle, so I added mine. The magazine article had used bolded subheads, so I did the same. Looking through I also saw they had used bulleted lists, so I knew it was okay to do the same. I followed the format until I completed my article. Then I looked at the author bio. It was only a short bio note of about 35 words. So, even though I wanted to tell the readers all about myself and provide a list of books, etc., I only wrote a 35-word bio at the end of my article. When I finished, I knew I had crafted an article that both satisfied the format of the publication I was targeting and provided readers with useful information in a familiar and palatable form.

Studying the markets is a process. The publishing world is a vast area with many different opportunities at your fingertips if you just know where to look.

Most magazines and websites have writers guidelines available to prospective writers. Securing guidelines for a magazine you want to write for is a must. Guidelines are available on magazine websites and by email upon request. An abbreviated version of the guidelines is available in market guides which we will discuss shortly.

When you are comparing guidelines, keep in mind the plan you have for the article. Is it compatible with the mission of the magazine? If not, do you want to change the slant of your article to make it fit? You may find more than one magazine is a possibility. If that happens you have a choice to make—1) Do you want to send it out to the first one on the list, wait for a reply, then if it is rejected, send it to the next one? Or 2) Do you want to send it to the first, then write a brand-new article using the same research and send to the next one on the list?

> A simultaneous submission to a magazine is a submission that you have offered to more than one magazine at the same time.

Either way works, and some writers believe in sending simultaneous submissions to magazines. A simultaneous submission to a magazine is a submission that you have offered to more than one magazine at the same time. If you do this, you must inform the magazine in your query letter that you are sending the same article at the same time to another magazine. Then if you receive an acceptance, you must notify all the other publishers the article is no longer available. While this works for some writers, others feel there is a lot of record keeping necessary to make sure you don't sell an article twice at the same time. The simultaneous submission of articles is probably not a good idea for beginning writers.

> An unsolicited manuscript is an article that the editor did not assign to someone or request to see.

138

When you read the guidelines, look for specific information. Do they accept unsolicited manuscripts? An unsolicited manuscript is an article that the editor did not assign to someone or request to see. It is sent to him or her with hopes he or she will read it and ultimately buy it.

Several advantages can help you get through the "gate" even when the guidelines state the magazine does not accept unsolicited manuscripts.

A well-written query letter. If you have written and asked to send your article and you have received a positive reply from the editor, your article no longer is unsolicited. You can send it immediately to the editor since he or she responded affirmatively to your query.

Meeting an editor at a writers conference. Most conferences offer 10-15-minute meetings as part of the tuition, although the time could be as short as 5-7 minutes. When you have a meeting with an editor to pitch your idea, you may receive a verbal green light to send your article to the magazine. This meeting bypasses even the query letter and gives you immediate permission to send your completed manuscript to the magazine.

A friend introduces you to an editor with whom you have a conversation about your article. This circumstance does not happen often.

Consider the word count. When magazines request a word count, they have a specific reason for wanting articles of that length. Usually, it involves how many words they can fit on the page when combined with other graphic elements.

"Pays on acceptance" means the magazine pays you when your article is accepted, and you have signed a contract. "Pays on publication" means when the article is published, you will receive a check.

Do not send them more words than the guidelines state. In the beginning, writers sometimes think, *Oh, if I go over by 150 words it won't matter because my words are so good they can't possibly turn them down.* Not so. Magazines usually leave some wiggle room in the requested word count so they can adjust and edit if necessary. But exceeding the requested word count is an easy rejection for an editor. When they receive a manuscript that doesn't fit the parameters listed in the guidelines, they immediately assume the writer has a hard time with boundaries.

The guidelines also tell you whether or not the editor accepts queries by email or if they still want you to snail mail your query. Pay close attention to the editor's preferred method and only use that one. If the magazine accepts email queries, remember this is still a formal business query to someone you have never met. Follow the rules of etiquette for a business letter. You can write it in a word document and then transfer over to your mail if you want the benefit of spell check and grammar check. If you have a letterhead, include it in your email query as well. Resist the urge to consider email the opportunity to be chatty and overly friendly with the editor, especially if you have never met him or her before. Even though email is a more relaxed form of communication, this **remains a** business query. When you have developed a relationship **with** an editor and you have written many articles for him or her, you may be able to relax your style slightly. If the magazine still requests snail-mail queries, don't forget to include an SASE (Self-addressed, stamped envelope) for the reply. That seems a little antiquated, and you may receive an email response, but including the SASE is still common practice. Some magazines still require snail-mail so be sure to check your target publication's practice.

Lead time is the amount of time the magazine needs to receive your article before publication.

Does the magazine pay on acceptance or on publication? This is an important question particularly if you are counting on the income from your article to pay the bills. "Pays on acceptance" means the magazine pays you when your article is accepted, and you have signed a contract. "Pays on publication" means when the article is published, you will receive a check. Since some magazines don't publish your article until a year or more after acceptance; it could be quite some time before you receive payment.

If you have a seasonal article, make a note of the lead time. Lead time is the amount of time the magazine needs to receive your article before publication. This varies from magazine to magazine so be sure to verify. Seasonal articles are among the most sought-after, especially if you have a fresh, new angle on the holiday.

Guidelines also provide a mailing address for your article and the magazine's preferred method of submission.

Most guidelines also list a response time. If you read their response time is four to six months, don't think your article will be the exception. Wait until the stated time has passed then add more time before you call or email inquiring about the status of your manuscript. Most magazine editors are busy and need time to go through all the articles sent to them. If you do inquire, make sure it is a friendly, polite, and low-key inquiry. The best way to use the time while you are waiting for a reply to a magazine submission is to get started on your next article.

The percentage of articles from first-time authors is listed in the guidelines. This number is helpful to new writers because they can assess their chances of publication with that magazine.

Another place to look for markets is to consult the printed market guides that are available. There are several available for purchase and also in the reference section of your local library.

The Writer's Market published annually by *Writer's Digest* is one of the best known. It is an expensive guide, but it is full of valuable information and well worth the investment. Having this guide on your bookshelf assures you always have many markets to choose from for your writing.

The beginning of the market guide often contains helpful articles on various subjects related to writers. These articles provide valuable information to help writers grow their skills and craft.

As you venture into the market guide, you see two major sections—one with book publishers and one for periodicals. For articles, you want to go directly to the periodical section where there are sections divided by topic.

Decide which topic your article fits under and turn to that section. Under each topic there are numerous magazines listed. For a first-time writer, the market guide can seem a bit overwhelming. It would be a good idea to start reading the periodicals section armed with sticky notes or a pen and notebook. There are so many magazines, many of which you have probably never heard of. Scan through the titles. Pay close attention to the types of articles they are looking for. Look at the length of articles they are looking for. Study the short paragraph about that magazine and see if it feels like a good fit. If you find one that might work, jot it down on your notebook or put a sticky note on the page.

EXPERT WORD

A few years back, a literary agency included this warning with his entry for the *Christian Writer's Market Guide*: "No exceptions. Don't ask to be the exception."

Editors everywhere share that frustration. There's a reason for each item in their guidelines. That's what they seek.

Imagine your frustration if you asked a clerk for a size eight silk, knee-length dress in teal—then were shown size 2 or 12, in mid-thigh or floor length, in orange or pink wool. Worse, to be told if you only prayed about it, those would be your first choice.

Too many writers think they can be the exception. Or they never take the trouble to check what the editor wants. Either way, they build their reputation.

So do writers who follow the rules: not only for the article's content but also for its format and how it's submitted. You can stand out from the crowd simply by following directions.

Andy Scheer, Andy Scheer Editorial Services
(www.andyscheer.com)

Decide which topic your article fits under and turn to that section. Under each topic there are numerous magazines listed. For a first-time writer, the market guide can seem a bit overwhelming. It would be a good idea to start reading the periodicals section armed with sticky notes or a pen and notebook. There are so many magazines, many of which you have probably never heard of. Scan through the titles. Pay close attention to the types of articles they are looking for. Look at the length of articles they are looking for. Study the short paragraph about that magazine and see if it feels like a good fit. If you find one that might work, jot it down on your notebook or put a sticky note on the page.

When you have narrowed your list, visit the websites of the magazines you think might be opportunities for you and download or order their writers guidelines. Many may have sample copies on the website where you can read and understand the style and voice of the magazine.

If your article is faith-based, you need a copy of the *Christian Writer's Market Guide.* It works similarly to the *Writer's Market* except the markets that are listed are from Christian publishers. They have the same needs as general market publishers, but there must be a faith element to your writing. Great opportunities abound in this area as well.

One addition to the *Christian Writers Market Guide* is the topical index. These pages of lists of subjects by topic are a gold mine for writers. When you know the topic you are going to write on or have written on, you can go to the topical index and find direction for marketing your work.

For instance, if you write an article titled "7 Ways to Help Your Child Sleep Better" you go to the topical index and look at the parenting entry. Underneath the parenting heading, you find several columns with names of magazines listed. All of those magazines accept parenting articles. Go to each magazine entry and scan to see if it is a fit for your article. Select the top five or so possibilities and go to their websites to check out their guidelines. Also look at issues of the magazine to make sure your article is a fit.

All the checking and rechecking of guidelines to find just the right market for your work may seem like a lot of work to you as you are starting out. However, this diligence on the front end saves you time in the long run. If you find the right market, your chances of rejection are less and therefore your time in marketing your article is less, and you are free to move on to your next project. And, as you study these markets, you are likely to come up with ideas leading to other articles. Be sure to keep a running list of all the possibilities.

If you are just starting out, you may want to look at the Sunday "take-home papers" some churches make available for the adults in their churches. Some of these publish monthly, but some of them publish a new issue every week. What does that mean to you as a writer? It means they need 52 issues worth of fresh, new materials. That is a lot of opportunity for writers. Some of the "take-home papers include Live, Seek, Purpose, Power for Living, etc. Some denominations have take-home papers for all ages.

The Christian Writers Market Guide also includes a special section on devotion markets, gifts, writers groups, writers conferences, contest, and agents.

You are probably wondering where to look for opportunities if you have exhausted opportunities in the market guides. Another great way is to request theme lists from magazines and determine if there is a fit for your type of writing.

Many magazines have a theme list. If so, make sure you pitch an article that works with the theme list. Theme lists are often on the website, but sometimes you may have to write and ask for the list. Editors have usually spent a lot of time developing the year's direction of the magazine and want to make sure articles fit within their themes.

Theme lists often coincide with seasons of the year, such as

January—New Beginnings
February—Love
March—Easter
April—Spring
May—Mother's Day
June—Father's Day
July—Independence
August—Back-to-School

September—Labor Day
October—Fall
November—Thanksgiving
December—Christmas.

The themes listed above seem fairly easy to guess. But what about other theme lists? Some religious magazines follow the liturgical calendar. General market magazines may follow the season for an overall theme, and the editorial team determines what is the best fit within those themes. Specialized magazines may use subjects within their readership interests.

Devozine, a teen, devotional lifestyle magazine of Upper Room Ministries has an extensive theme list published on their website. This list directs writers to the major categories for each issue and elaborates in the form of questions to encourage thinking and creativity in the writing of the articles. You can find the list at http://devozine.upperroom.org/write-for-us/themes/. Even if you end up not submitting to this magazine, the *Devozine* theme list is thought-provoking and gets your creative juices flowing.

Media kits are another good place to look for ideas. Many magazines, especially the larger ones have media kits available online. You may have to look at the small print lists at the bottom of the page to find them or use the search box to find them. Writers are not always aware this information is available to them. But sometimes it is just a matter of looking in the right place.

The *First for Women* 2017 media kit is about twenty pages of information about the Bauer Media Group, their publications, and their needs. Several pages are devoted to the demographics of their readers as well as their shopping and reading habits. A chart compares their sales to other women's magazines which is helpful information. Then buried in the middle of the media kit, is their editorial theme list for the year. I have only to look at those pages to find the issue number, on-sale date, the overall theme for the issue and what they're looking for broken down by departments. All of the department needs relate to the issue theme. These suggestions of what they're looking for gives writers a good idea of where to target their ideas if they want to pitch to the *First for Women* magazine.

Parents magazine is another popular magazine for families with children. If you are a writer with children, you are probably daily living situations that would make great articles. Before you get excited about the most creative birthday party you have ever executed for a five-year-old, you should check their theme list and see if perhaps birthday parties is one of their editorial targets. As with the magazine for women above, *Parents* lists the monthly theme then breaks their needs into subjects by departments.

> A niche market is a specialized part of a subject about which you have become an expert at writing.

If you can locate the media kit for a magazine you want to write for, you are a step ahead. You know the demographic of the reader you are writing for. You understand a bit more of the philosophy and mission statement of the magazine and why they exist. You also know how their advertising works and who their advertisers are. And you may find new markets within the pages of the media kits. Many of the larger media groups have more than one publication and usually at least mention them in the media kit. Doing an online search for the name of the magazine leads you to the parent company or media group.

Where to find opportunities?

Word of mouth is an excellent way to find article markets. Friends who are writers can often direct you. Join Facebook groups, both general market and those specifically for your niche market.

What's a niche market? A niche market is a specialized part of a subject about which you have become an expert at writing. A good place to find your niche is to look at former employment and hobbies. What have you done in years past that others would be interested in? Have you been a teacher? Have you served in the Peace Corps? Have you worked as a team leader in a successful business?

When you begin to write multiple articles about one subject, readers tend to look at you as the expert. If they are curious about your subject, they eagerly await your next article and perhaps even hope for a book someday.

Just because you begin writing for a niche market doesn't mean you have to stay there forever. Some writers begin with one area and then branch out to another area or even more. Writing for a niche market is beneficial to writers because when you establish yourself in that area, you are sought after for your expertise.

New Magazines

Watch the newsstand and internet for magazines just getting started. When a magazine begins publication, it doesn't have the benefit of a long list of writers who have written for them before. Opportunities abound for new writers.

When you discover a new magazine, quickly do your detective work. Find out who the editor is, who the parent company is, what their focus is, who their readers are, what information is on their websites such as a media kit, writers guidelines, or theme list. Read the first issue to determine the voice of the magazine. Take note of their advertisers.

When you have done all that, you are ready to come up with an idea fitting their target readership. Develop your idea well according to the style of the magazine and submit. Even if your first article doesn't get accepted, keep in mind you are building a relationship with the editor. If you feel the magazine is a good fit for you, keep submitting. If the editor has given you feedback, pay close attention to what he or she says and act on his or her advice.

EXPERT WORD

When a new Christian magazine came to town, I knew I wanted to write for it. I studied the different features and submitted an article I thought would fit well. The editor accepted it, but informed me she couldn't pay me for my submission. At that point in my professional journey, I was working hard at building my writing resume, so I was just happy to add another print publishing credit.

A few months later, I wrote another piece and submitted it. Again the editor accepted it. Still no payment, but now I had another article to my credit.

Two months after that, the editor contacted me. "There's an event happening in your neighborhood," she said. "We need a writer to cover it. Would you be interested?" Would I? You bet. I did the happy dance later that month when I received a (small) check in the mail.

As I continued to prove I could write well, meet deadlines, and accept editing suggestions, my editor gave me more and more paid assignments. When she received a three-book contract and had to resign her editorship, guess who she recommended to replace her? Me.

Does it pay to give your writing away? Absolutely. If you approach it as an internship, even if it doesn't translate into a paid position, you'll have learned a lot, gained writing credits for your resume, and built valuable relationships in the publishing world.

Lori Hatcher, Editor, Reach Out, Columbia magazine
(www.ReachOutColumbia.com)

Bookstores

Bookstores are another great place for research. Granted not all bookstores carry a lot of magazines. But some have an entire wall of periodicals. Many have comfy chairs nearby.

There are several ways you can approach this. First, you can go to the bookstore, find your chair for the morning and methodically work down the magazine rack. This works best when you want to browse, catch up on the trending stories, and get your creative juices flowing. Second, if you already have an idea perking in the brain, then you need to check out all the possible magazines. As you browse through those, make a list of the articles you could write on your subject idea and how you could slant the information differently. Then you have multiple articles to begin.

Online opportunities

You can also find well-paying opportunities by doing an online search. There are several ways you can locate markets online as well as the websites of print magazines.

If you know the publication's name you would like to write for, simply search for that magazine. You will probably be taken to their website where you can search for their guidelines, editorial calendars, theme lists, sample articles, and more.

If you are just not sure where your idea would fit, try a general search for writing opportunities in your area of expertise. Try putting "submissions + philanthropy" in the search box if that is your subject. If that doesn't yield any prospects, put "write for us + sports medicine." "Writing opportunities + your subject" is another way you can search. This type search should give you several opportunities that will at least be the beginnings of tracking down a good writing opportunity.

Online job boards are another place you can find opportunities for writing articles. A popular one is craigslist.com. Type your location and then check writing in the jobs column. Another popular site is allfreelancewriting.com. There you find a variety of writing jobs posted, where they are, the rate of pay, etc. Other job listings are on upwork.com, freelancer.com, freelancewriting.com, mediabistro.com, bloggingpro.com. As you can see, there are lots of places to look for freelance article work, and I have only listed a few of them. As always with online resources, you should frequently check to make sure they are still operating and up to date. As of this writing, all of the above are live and have numerous job postings. A few of them charge for their services, but many do not.

Look for Facebook groups in your writing specialty area. They often post opportunities and at the very least provide good conversation with others who share your writing passion.

Job opportunities for writing for newsletters are also online. Some of these sites are for articles, and others are for writing jobs. One of these sites is Morning Coffee Newsletter put out by freelancewriting. com, and there is one called freelancewritinggigs.com. They bring writing opportunities right into your mailbox.

Writing Newspaper Articles

Many writers think because newspapers have paid staffs they don't need freelance writers. Most newspapers are open to freelance even if they don't make that fact widely known. They are aware that different writers have different perspectives and different world views and can bring value to their publications.

If you want to write for a newspaper, keep your eyes open for a story that might be of interest to their readers. Check the circulation area of the newspaper so you are aware of the location of their readership. Some newspapers serve only a local area, some are regional, and others are national. Start out with the smaller papers unless you already have a national presence.

Watch for unique events, people who are coming to town, or unusual natural phenomena. Remember those high-profile events have already had lots of publicity and have most likely already caught the newspaper editor's eye. For local and regional papers, human interest is a significant factor and one they don't always hear about. If you can provide warm and fuzzy stories about one or more residents, you may find an opening for your writing.

Newspapers are a good market for writers. Keep in mind the turnaround time is short and the story must be tightly written. Pay is usually minimal or nonexistent at the local level, especially for writers who are writing for the newspaper for the first time.

Compilation Books

Compilation books have been popular for a long time. A compilation book is a collection of articles and/or stories written by different authors. This type book often issues calls for submissions on the internet or on their websites. If you want to find opportunities to submit to these publications, do a search for "call for submissions for compilation books." You will probably be surprised at how many there are and how many different themes and subjects are available.

One of the most popular compilation books is *Chicken Soup for the Soul*. You can find what they are looking for by visiting www.chickensoup.com. If you look at the tab, "Submit Your Story," you find a listing of possible book topics. There is a detailed description of what they are looking for as well as a tab for their guidelines.

Articles are a great way to promote and market your book even before you have a book in print.

Compilation books have different guidelines and also buy different rights. When you are signing a contract to place your article in a compilation book, take note of the rights they are purchasing. Many compilation books used to buy all rights. These days fewer are buying all rights, but since some do, you must carefully read the contract section on rights. Today many of these books buy first rights. If they buy first rights, make sure you know when the rights revert to you. There is sometimes a waiting period before you can offer your article to another publication. Some magazines and compilation books state 60 days, others 90, and others have no waiting period at all.

Chapter 12
Articles—Great Way to Market Books and Build your Platform

"The best time to start promoting your book is three years before it comes out," writes Seth Godin on his blog. Three years to build a reputation, build a permission asset, build a blog, build a following, build credibility and build the connections you'll need later." If that's the case, how in the world are you supposed to promote a book three years in advance? By writing articles.

Articles are a great way to promote and market your book even before you have a book in print. Writing articles on the subject of your book helps you build your platform and establish yourself as an expert in the subject field. The broader the audience you reach with articles, the wider your potential book audience. Articles connect your book to many different sources for possible sales.

Don't limit yourself to one area of your book's coverage. For example, if your book is about collecting vintage clothing, don't limit yourself to writing about vintage clothing. When you have adequately covered the subject of clothing, you might branch out to talk about the people who wore that clothing. Your research on people of a certain era certainly acquaints you with their habits and way of family life. Or perhaps you might discover other collectibles from the same time periods and write about that. You could go in many different directions from your one vintage clothing collection book. As you write about the clothing and the related subjects, you establish yourself as one who is very knowledgeable in that area.

EXPERT WORD

When I finish and send in that first draft to the editor, the next thing I do is make a list of all the blogs and articles I can write that would help and assist a reader, but it is also woven in with the theme of my book. So, readers not only benefit from something that helps in his or her life, but it is also a teaser for them to take a look at my next novel.

For example, in my next book, *High Treason*, I have written a blog and an article about how to get along with difficult people, how to approach people of different cultures when you want to befriend them. And, of course, how to impact people for the Kingdom with your faith when they believe differently from you.

My article, "10 Characteristics of a Strong Woman," discusses the characteristics of a strong woman. What does that mean, especially to a woman who embraces Jesus? "Getting over the Past," addresses continually blaming ourselves for things that happened in the past, how to forgive ourselves and move forward. Those are themes in my book, and all of those are things that we deal with.

DiAnn Mills, www.DiAnnMills.com

You may be wondering about the novel you are working so hard to complete. How could you possibly use articles to promote fiction? Do any of your characters have special issues? Is the theme of your novel related to a life season? Is the genre you are writing appealing to one age group or another?

For example, suppose the main character in your novel is a special needs child who has been bullied at school. Right there, you have two huge subjects that you can write about. You could write about special needs children and how to parent them using your character's parenting style as an illustration. Or you might explore the all-too-common issue of bullying. Does it just happen to special needs children? Are there certain ages that bully or are bullied more than others? How can you prevent bullying? What should the school system do to prevent bullying in the schools? What about cyberbullying? See what happens when you start to let your mind wander around the issues of your book.

Nonfiction books and novels often open the doors for opportunities to write articles just as articles provide opportunities to promote your book. Almost every article you write needs to have a bio attached. When you write that bio that has a connection to your book, you simply state, "Mary Jones is a freelance writer for many publications and the author of the soon-to-be-released book, *Vintage Clothing Collections—A Special Hobby.*" Including your book in your bio gets the word out to many people and begins to connect your name with the name of your book.

Another exciting part of using articles as a marketing tool is that most magazines are read by thousands if not millions of people. Therefore, when your article reaches that many people, you have also introduced your book and your subject to a tremendous number of potential readers. Since most books do well to sell 1,000 copies on their own, writing articles can boost sales as well as extend the reach of your message.

Carefully choosing your magazine markets also introduces your book to potential readers by connecting your name with the magazine they read regularly. Locating all the specific trade journals and consumer publications that relate to your subject just increases your readership pool.

Hiring a publicist is an option for writers today, but most writers find that large investment not to be in their budgets. These days even publishers are not able to keep full-time publicists on staff. And if they have a publicist, he or she is probably one person working for the good of many authors. Often that person is happy to meet with you when needed to develop a plan for marketing your book. But the actual work of implementing your marketing plan is up to you.

A local writing organization sponsored an evening at the library. They brought in several successful New York City authors and another from a different state. These folks all had books already in print and others in the works. The evening format was a panel discussion where the moderator guided a discussion and then the floor was open for questions. After the discussion, the first question was, "Can you tell me a little bit about writing articles? How can I start doing that?"

There was a pronounced hush on the panel. They all looked around not daring to make eye contact with the moderator. Finally, she said, "Sam, what about you? Could you address that question please?"

Sam cleared his throat. "I really don't write articles."

The moderator looked at the next person on the panel. "Margie?"

Margie just shrugged her shoulders.

The next panelist answered before the moderator even asked. "I have never written an article. That might be very interesting."

The moderator looked at the audience and closed out the session. "I guess we aren't able to help you. None of us have ever written articles."

I sat at the back of the room, and my mouth was open way too long. These high-profile writers had never considered using articles as a way to build their platforms and promote their books? How much greater the reach of their messages could be, yet they had never even thought about writing an article.

For that reason, you need to do everything you can to get the word out about your book. Articles are an excellent way to do that. And the best time to do that is, as Seth Godin says, before your book is at the publisher, even three years before.

AUTHOR NOTE

When my first book came out, I was regularly writing articles for *Focus on the Family*. Most of the articles were related to parenting which was the theme of my first book, *Love Notes in Lunchboxes*. I always made sure to include mention of the new book in my bio. Because of one of my articles, I was asked to be on their radio show. We talked about a lot of subjects during the half-hour radio show. Of course, when they introduced me they mentioned the name of my book and again at the end. What happened regarding getting the word out about my book? Let's do the math.

Published article in magazine	1,000,000 readers
Magazines are passed around 3-7 times	3-7,000,000 additional readers
Radio show	222,000,000 listeners
Total	**226-231,000,000 people**

Not bad publicity for my book, especially considering I didn't have to pay anything but got paid along the way for my article. That's a win-win!

EXPERT WORD

Is it necessary to write articles first? Necessary isn't the word I'd use; I would say it's wise.

Starting with articles accomplishes several things before you attempt to write a book.

You prove to a book editor you are publishable.

You gain needed writing credits.

You make more money, something no writer has ever rejected.

Cec Murphey, award-winning author,
speaker, and mentor to many

Chapter 13
The Business Side of Writing

Along with publishing articles comes your exciting contract written entirely in lawyerese. What do you need to do? You may ask yourself how you will ever understand what all those words mean.

Most article contracts are shorter than book contracts. Nevertheless, for your first contract, you should have someone go over the contract and help you decipher all the terms. The person could be a literary attorney if you so choose, but every town doesn't not have a literary attorney. And, not all attorneys are familiar with literary contracts. Find a writer friend perhaps in your writers group who has some experience with article contracts. He or she can help you and explain some of the terms new to you. You can also hire someone in the writing business who frequently helps people negotiate contracts.

A contract lists the title of the article the publisher is buying, the word count, due date, rights purchased, payment, and timing of payment. Some magazines pay on acceptance while others pay on publication. For the writer, paying on acceptance is preferable because you get your payment right away when the article has been accepted. Paying on publication means you are paid when the article is published. Waiting until your article is published could mean you are not paid for a long time, at least the length of the lead time of the magazine. If a natural disaster or holiday preempts the original publication date, the article could be bumped and held even longer before it is in print which, in turn, extends the wait for payment.

Some magazines don't use contracts and writers just receive an email containing all the same terms you would find in a contract.

Read your contract carefully to make sure there are not any terms you don't understand. For instance, years ago when the internet first became popular, some contracts contained the offer of a little extra money for web rights. Now somewhere in the article contract it probably discusses web rights and sometimes other rights are included in the payment offered. Since most magazines now have websites, it makes sense they would want articles they buy to do double duty. Having both a print and digital outlet is also a plus for writers because some magazines, *Country Living, Family Circle*, and *Women's Day* just to name a few, buy additional content (articles) for their websites. Sometimes the payment is different, but some pay the same thing for articles whether they use them in print or digitally.

Some people ask, "Can you negotiate an articles contract?" The simple answer is not usually, especially if it is your first time writing for that magazine. As you become more published, you can set payment standards. If a magazine doesn't want to adjust their pay scale, then you are free to look elsewhere to place your article.

Reprints

Getting your articles back into circulation in the reprint world is an important part of the **business side of writing**. Reprints require little additional work, just **a dusting** off, updating any personal information, and getting them in the mail or email.

We touched on the subject of reprints a bit in the section about rights. Reprint rights are essential to writers for a lot of reasons, but especially because selling reprint rights has the potential to generate additional income for the writer while not requiring

> Reprints require little additional work, just a dusting off, updating any personal information, and getting them in the mail or email.

a lot of extra work hours. When your article is in print and the rights are yours again (check your contract for the exact amount of time you must wait), you are free to sell your work as a reprint. It is not necessary to change it in any way if you are offering it as a reprint. In fact, for your article to be a reprint, it must be exactly as it was when published.

If you want to sell reprint rights, it is very simple. If you are mailing your article to another magazine as a reprint, you can make a copy of the printed article along with a copy of the cover of the magazine and send those to the new magazine. Be sure to send your contact information. If you send your article by email, you can attach your original manuscript with only a few minor changes. The most significant difference would be to change the rights you are offering. The first time you published you offered first rights. This time you are offering reprint rights. Under the rights line on the right side of your paper, type, "First appeared in (Name of the magazine) then the date." Then the new publisher can locate the issue where your article was first published.

Since you are offering reprint rights, you can send it to many magazines at a time. However, it is best not to send it to competing markets at the same time. Competing markets are those which serve the same or similar readerships. Regional magazines, state magazines, and denominational magazines are three of the best known noncompeting markets, and many of them accept **reprints**.

Competing markets are those which serve the same or similar readerships.

Business Cards and Other Correspondence Materials

As every good business person knows, contact information is important. Business cards for a writer don't have to be elaborate. It is a good idea to put your photograph on your business card, especially if you plan to attend conferences and meet with editors who meet with many different people. Your photo helps them remember you. If you have a tagline, you may want to include that on your card.

A word of caution. Only include the information someone would need to hire you as a writer or purchase an article from you. Home address and phone number are not necessary. If you want to include an address, rent a post office box near your home. If you want to have a telephone number on your card, check out some of the free internet number services that feed directly into your business number. Personal information is not necessary or a good idea.

Also buy stationery with your business logo, personalized notecards, and other such materials to keep on hand. Even though you may work from your home, you should be prepared to have the same professional look as any other business.

Office Upkeep

Your writing business needs to have a supply area where you keep envelopes, stamps, paper clips, printer ink, sticky notes, pens and pencils, scissors, and anything else you might need. Make sure your chair has excellent support and desk is big enough to hold all your project material and research.

Contact File

Any time you meet a new writer, editor, or agent ask for a business card. In the writing world, contacts are gold. Writers must be networkers, and often you find help among those you have met at conferences.

Find a good system that works for you. Some people like to save cards in a notebook or physical file. Others digitally scan the cards and keep them in a folder on the computer. A very easy app to use is CamCard. It scans the entire business card and puts it in a folder conveniently accessible at any time.

When someone gives you his or her card and you sense he or she will be a good contact down the road, make a few notes on the card to jog your memory regarding your connection. For instance, if you write mystery novels and you meet someone who is a retired private investigator, ask him or her if you may email questions if you come to a place in your writing where you need help. It is amazing how much we can help each other if we keep our contact information updated.

AUTHOR NOTE

On the first day of a class I was teaching at a technical college we went around the room introducing ourselves and telling a bit about our writing. We came to a man on the front row, and he introduced himself as a retired policeman. A lady several rows back jumped to her feet, pointed at him, and repeated loudly, "I need you, I need you."

She was writing a crime novel and had hit a roadblock. She wanted to know if she had used the proper method to kill the victim in her work. They exchanged cards after spending quite a bit of time chatting about her method of murder!

Perhaps you are a spreadsheet person. Keeping all your networking information on a spreadsheet is another good way to keep track of contacts. Make sure you have a column for the occupation/interests of your networking community.

When you treat your writing as a business, you begin to think of yourself as a professional and find your way in the publishing world.

Chapter 14
Setting Goals for Your Writing

Setting goals for your writing career is a bit like taking a trip. You must know where you are going and create a plan for getting there. Then it is simple. You follow your "roadmap."

With a plan, you focus more intently on your goal and are much less likely to get off track. Having a plan for your writing gives you a target to aim for and self-imposed deadlines. Goals provide you with purpose and strategy for reaching your deadlines. When you work in the solitude of home, you don't have anyone around reminding you of milestones toward your goal. Accountability from others is limited so having a map or checklist helps bring accountability to your day.

AUTHOR NOTE

When I was a little girl, my father decided part of our growing-up, educational experience should be a road trip across the United States. One summer we packed the car, tied the suitcases on top, and climbed in. Before starting the car, Daddy said, "I have a roadmap for each one of you so you can follow our route. Here are highlighters and you can mark off each part of the trip. You can watch as we get closer to our destination. This is going to be a great family time!"

It looked like a long way from South Carolina to California, but we found marking off the trip one interstate at a time not only made the distance go quickly but also made it feel possible to get there.

Several actions help you move forward toward your goal.

- Write your goals. Unless you know what you are trying to accomplish, you can't hone your plan for success. Writing your goals on paper gives you a concrete procedure to follow. You can't work the plan if you don't have one you can refer to so write it down. For some, making a goal list means making a new file on your computer where you always have it at your fingertips. Set reminders along the way to check your progress. For others who use a physical planner, goals must be included in your monthly lists so you can track your progress. Choose what works best for you. Break your goals into manageable parts. As you meet each deadline on the way to your goal, you find success and are encouraged to keep on track.

- Prioritize your goals according to the deadline date, research required, or personal preference. Some people prefer to do all their research at one time while others like to check the steps off one at a time for each project. Full-time writers may want to set weekly goals. If you are just getting started or writing in your spare time, monthly listings may work. Remember as you set your goals to include all areas of your writing life, not only actual writing time.

Writing takes a lot of your time. Writing includes computer writing but also counts your research, interviews, and working on the foundation of your writing career.

Submitting is included in your writing time. A realistic goal for submissions keeps you in reach of success. If you write full-time, perhaps the realistic workload for you would include several articles a week. If you are just getting your writing career off the ground, maybe one or two submissions a month is more realistic.

Creating effective query letters and book proposals is submission time well spent. And sending out reprint articles can be an easy way to increase the income from one article.

Occasionally, following up on a submitted article is necessary.

Always be on the lookout for new markets. Study them constantly as they often change.

Don't get stuck writing for only one or two magazines. Find creative ways to market your articles and connect them to special events. Read and study possible periodical markets. Write or search the internet for guidelines.

During your business time, you invoice, make new contacts, take care of correspondence—anything in the business of writing category. Also during this time, make sure your printer has plenty of ink, your paper cabinet is stocked, and you have plenty of supplies.

Writers are constantly learning. Make time for writer's conferences, online communication with other writers, and join a critique group. Set a goal to read at least one writing book a month. Take a course at a local university or community college.

Be specific about your goals. Instead of "Write one book this year," add to your list "Send proposal on the book *How to Publish 500 Articles Per Year* to Publisher X, Publisher Y, and Publisher Z within the next six months. If you only have a seed of an idea, describe your idea in as much detail as possible. Specific goals help eliminate mental wandering and keep you focused on your target.

Set attainable goals

For example, if you are a stay-at-home mom taking care of three toddlers and an elderly parent who requires constant supervision, you probably cannot expect to write three novels a year or even two articles a week. Or if you are a waitress and work at a restaurant 60+ hours a week, you may not have a lot of free time to write. Give yourself the opportunity for success by planning realistically.

If you only aim for what is easily within reach, you won't stretch and grow as a writer. You need to focus on your energy and discipline. Even if you don't reach the top goal you have set for your writing, the journey in pursuit of the highest goal will make you a better writer.

- Post a list where you see it every day.

- Tape it above your computer, write it on your desktop

screen, or purchase a whiteboard to use for your goal posting. Seeing the list often helps keep you focused. And knowing you have a custom plan gives you the freedom to dream and to include every little whim.

- Don't broadcast your goals.

    This "road map" is for you only. Others will only see it if you share. Review your list frequently. Very few activities (except maybe opening the envelope containing the check!) bring you more satisfaction than checking a completed project off your list.

When you achieve a goal, celebrate. Go out to dinner or cook a special meal if you have neglected the kitchen while writing. Play with your children or take them to a movie they have wanted to see, go out to lunch with a friend. Take a long hot bath and read a book. Your self-confidence spurs you on as you move on to your next goal. Savor the moment!

Now review your list. What is the next goal on the list? Are you ready to work on it or has another idea risen to the top? Did you learn something in completing this goal that affects one of the others? Were the goals too easy? Too hard? Did you discover an area of weakness in your writing?

Your goals may change. They are not written in stone. As your writing skills improve, opportunities may arise to add to your list or possibly may preempt another item. Be flexible if you feel you need to revise your goals.

Don't be too hard on yourself if you don't reach a goal. Failure is not an end. Failure can be a great teacher. Assess where you missed the mark, reevaluate your goals, and get back to work.

Ronald Reagan said, "My philosophy of life is that if we make up our minds what we are going to make of our lives, then work hard toward that goal, we never lose – somehow we always win out." He would probably advise all writers to set those goals high and never lose site of the purpose of their work. And even if the path to that goal changes, there is great value in the lessons learned along the way.

What does your "roadmap" for your writing look like? Do you need to start at the beginning and create one? Grab a pencil and paper and put on your "dreaming cap."

Keep Learning

Writers never "arrive." There are always new subjects to explore and new markets to discover. And, just as you think you have figured out the publishing industry, it changes again. For those reasons and more, writers are lifelong learners.

With the advent of the digital age, many magazines began digital editions and eventually eliminated the print version. More join the trend each year. New all-digital publications are started. Editors seem to move around a lot, often from one publication to another. Yet another reason you should carefully check before you submit. Know the state of the magazine. Make sure you get the editor's name correct. Read the mission or purpose statement to make sure you are sending them something within the realm of what they are looking for.

Writers Conferences

Writers conferences are an excellent way for writers to continue learning. Some are hesitant to go to a writers conference because they feel they are very expensive or they may not know anyone else going. Writers conferences are important. Conferences are an investment in your writing career and offer so much more in one location than anywhere else. And even if you don't know anyone when you arrive, you are sure to make new friends at the conference and develop an entirely new network of support and encouragement for your writing.

Conference workshops are varied and provide learning in many areas of writing. Often they cover the basics of writing for publication and encourage writers who are beginning to write. Many conferences offer instruction for advanced writers as well. Before you sign up, make sure the conference you have chosen is going to provide the information you are looking for.

Some conferences are genre specific. They are for specific types of writing. There are conferences for children's writers, horror writers, nonfiction, fiction, writers of YA, and many more. Other conferences offer a little bit of everything. So, choose carefully. Take advantage of the workshops for all genres, networking with other writers, and opportunities to speak personally with editors, publishers, and agents.

One new trend is a one-day seminar for writers. Several writers travel around together to spend a day teaching writers in different areas of the country. Most of the time these are a great value for your money and provide you with lots of information about the craft of writing as well as keeping you up to date on the trends in the publishing business. Watch newspapers, Facebook, and other online advertisements for news of this type of learning experience.

Podcasts and Videos

Podcasts are another excellent way to learn about writing and writing opportunities. Some podcasts can be purchased for a small fee; others are free. Writers conferences record the sessions so you can benefit from the teaching even if you are not able to attend.

Search youtube.com, and you find videos of instructions for various types of articles. Go to the site and put in the subject you would like to learn about and you may be surprised at how many videos pop up.

A word of caution here. Anyone can make a podcast or YouTube video and post it. Make sure the ones you view or listen to are made by seasoned writers with proper credentials and ample experience.

Working with Editors

Editors are a writer's best friend. But too often writers don't see it that way. They put editors on a pedestal and become very nervous when they have the opportunity to speak with an editor. Keep in mind editors are people just like you. Their job just happens to be that of an editor.

The publishing business is comprised of many parts. Editors are dependent on writers to provide material for their publications and websites. Similarly, writers depend on editors to like their material so they can get published. You can help your editor by putting any fear aside and approaching editors with confidence and respect.

Writers conferences are a great place to connect with editors of many genres. When you are a considering a conference, carefully study the names of the editors who are attending. Make sure at least a few are looking for articles of the type you are writing. Read and study their publications before you get to the conference so you know what kind of articles they need and can ask questions intelligently.

When talking to an editor, remember:

- You are on the same team.

- He or she is just like you only God has called him or her to be an editor and you to be a writer.

- Your conversation will go much more smoothly if you do your "homework" before you meet.

- Connecting with his or her heart is of the utmost importance.

AUTHOR NOTE

At my first writer's conference, my greatest fear was I would have to speak with an editor face to face. Being pretty shy and not knowing what to say to someone I held in such high esteem, I was afraid to have any conversations with editors. Since I had never talked to an editor before, I felt would probably say all the wrong things.

One night at supper I arrived early. I saw the editor I had submitted one of my manuscripts to. He spotted me and headed my way. I wanted to retreat to the safety of my room, but it was too late. I smiled.

He walked up to me and said, "You know I used to skip stones when I was a little boy."

My article was about watching my son skipping stones on a lake and the application to life.

There was my first lesson in my first encounter with an editor—connect with the editor's heart. I quickly learned my first goal should be to connect with the editor's heart. If you can't make that connection, you lose the opportunity to connect with your readers' hearts.

Another thing I learned: editors were like us. They were little boys and girls once, and I should be able to have a conversation with them just as I would with any other adult even though I was talking business instead of a casual conversation.

Not until the end of the conversation did this editor mention my writing. Then he said very little. He continued to tell me about his experience skipping stones as a little boy and what fun he had. The heart connection I had established with my article was much stronger than the impression I had made as a writer.

From then on I was always mindful of the importance of the editor/reader connection. The writing was a way to touch hearts to make a difference. What a great early lesson in writing to always write to a specific audience to change lives.

Chapter 15
Where to Go from Here

Now you have the how-to information and have set goals for your writing, where do you go from here? Here is a plan to help you get started.

Writing

Place your goal sheet in a prominent place.

Make sure you have access to a computer so you can put your thoughts on paper.

Look at the list of ideas you have made while reading this book.

Decide which idea you are most passionate about.

Begin the process of researching, outlining, writing, and marketing.

Remember perfecting each of the article types takes time and practice. Choose the one most appealing to you and start there. Take each step slowly so you can learn the basics as you go.

Find a writing mentor who can walk beside you as you learn.

EXPERT WORD

Every writer needs a mentor and every mentor needs a mentor as well. As a mentor, you can be a bridge between generations. You can change the world one writer at a time. In the 21st century mentoring or coaching is huge.

Edna Ellison, former magazine editor www.ednaellison.com

Growing as a Writer

Find a writers group you can join. Many communities have writers groups meeting regularly. Look in the back of market guides, search the Internet, and ask other writers to share information about groups they know. Some groups are specialized so look for one that focuses on the genre you write.

If there is no group in your community, join an online group. There are many, and some concentrate, on critiquing, others on instruction, and some combine both.

Attend a writers conference. There are writers conferences of all sizes, in many locations of the country, and with many different focuses. Choose wisely as to which conference may be the most beneficial for you. Study the faculty and see who will be there. If you are trying to market magazine articles, make sure there is an ample offering of magazine editors. Book editors and agents are always willing to chat with you about your work, but if you want to make a sale, you have to talk to the magazine editors who can buy your work.

Writers conferences often feel like huge expenditures. Attending those events are an investment in your writing career, and you should remember the benefits go far beyond a few days away from home. The contacts you make and the networking you establish will serve you long beyond your return home.

Many writers groups sponsor one-day writers seminars where they focus on one specific genre of writing. These day-long workshops are affordable and provide the opportunity for ongoing training for writers. Take advantage of as many of these a possible.

Local libraries sponsor workshops and groups for writers. Check with yours to see what opportunities are there.

Finally, remember to keep your priorities in order. Yes, sometimes deadlines mean you have to close yourself in a room to finish your article on time. But try to plan your writing to leave plenty of time for family. They only appreciate what you do if it doesn't interfere with their time with you.

You can do this. You can be a successful writer. If this is your first endeavor into the writing world, hang in there and work hard. If you have been writing for a while, pick a new type of article from this book and give it a try. You have something important to say, and many people need to read your words.

Revisit your motive for writing. If writing is not your passion, that's okay. Discover what you want to do and head to that path. The nice thing about writing is you can write articles as a complement to every other profession. But if you have discovered writing is your passion, learn all you can and put it into practice today.

Take Martin Luther's advice to heart, "If you want to change the world, pick up a pen."

Appendix

Article Check List

☑ Did I read the guidelines so I know what the publication is looking for?

☑ Did I follow the guidelines exactly?

☑ Do I know my target audience?

☑ Did I stick to my main point?

☑ Did I use fiction techniques to keep my writing lively and interesting?

☑ Did I edit my manuscript or ask a friend to do it for me?

☑ Is my writing conversational and reader friendly?

☑ Was my hook grabbing?

☑ Is my takeaway for the reader strong?

☑ Have I captured the reader's interest?

☑ Are transitions smooth and appropriate?

☑ Does my writing flow?

☑ Have I avoided clichés and slang?

☑ Does the article come to a strong conclusion?

☑ Are there redundancies?

☑ Can it be tightened?

☑ Have I read it aloud? Does it read smoothly?

☑ Have I checked grammar? Spelling? Readability?

Q & A with the Author

Question: This sounds good when you put it down on paper, but is it possible for a new writer to find a market interested in his or her work?

Answer: Absolutely. Of course, you must write your article well and in the voice of the publication you are trying to break into. But if you follow the guidelines of the magazine with no deviations to the guidelines and your writing is strong, your article certainly has a great chance of being considered by the magazine editor.

Question: How long should I wait before I follow up with the editor?

Answer: Most guidelines will tell you the response time of the editor. Do not contact an editor before the time has passed. In fact, it would be good to wait an extra week or two before you follow up. When you do, be sure to do it in a polite and non-nagging way. There are times when manuscripts do get lost or never make it to the magazine in the first place.

Question: If I have submitted a manuscript to an editor and I think of another idea for that magazine before I hear a response from the editor, is it okay to send a second submission?

Answer: You can if you want to. But if this is a new market for you, it might be a good idea to wait until you hear from the editor. You may need to tweak your voice a bit and rather than do it twice, just be patient. It is never a bad idea to keep submitting. So, when you send the first article in, write one for a different market. Then you will hear back from two editors and potentially will find two new markets for your work at the same time.

Question: Can you suggest a good beginner's market?

Answer: First of all, most magazines would not consider themselves beginner's markets. They look for top quality writing no matter what their circulation or frequency of publication. However, a good place to start is local or neighborhood magazines. Writing an article or two for them gives you practice in using proper format and meeting deadlines. Then you can move to other magazine formats. In the inspirational market, take home papers are a good starting place because their articles are short and many publish every week. If you learn the craft of writing and can submit proper articles, you will move quickly to larger magazines.

Question: I want to write for the really big magazines such as *Forbes, Good Housekeeping, or Time.* How do I find how to break into those markets?

Answer: Those markets are difficult to break in to but not impossible. It's best to have a few articles published before you even think of querying the big magazines. Regularly read the ones you want to write for so you are familiar with what they publish and the voice of the magazine. Read their guidelines and theme lists if they have them. Pay attention to the subjects they cover and how thoroughly they cover them. When you see a gap you might fill, write a persuasive query as to how you can fill that gap.

Question: You said earlier the first paragraph of your query might be the first paragraph of your article. Really? I just move the first paragraph of the query to the first paragraph of the article and go from there?

Answer: In a lot of cases, yes, that is exactly what you do. If you have spent time carefully writing the opening paragraph of your query, it can become the opening of your article. It hooked the editor in the query, didn't it? You may have to do a little tweaking, but if it is catchy and draws your editor in, it should do the same thing for the publisher.

Question: I often hear the word content associated with writing. What exactly is content?

Answer: Content is the collective name given to articles written for websites, blogs, newsletters, business communications and advertisements, and more for a specific audience. Chances are if you have written many articles, many may be in the content area. Content writers write for other people for their websites, blogs, or newsletters. Content writing educates, instructs, and entertains the reader. Content marketing is another type of content used to introduce the reader to a product or service in a way to make the reader want to know more about the product or even purchase it.

Have a question not listed? Email the author and ask her at linda@lindagilden.com. Be sure to put "Articles question" in the subject line.

Resources

Books

Finding Success with Your Dream Writing Projects by Dennis Hensley (Bold Vision Books, 2017) ISBN-10: 0997851481

Called to Write by Edna Ellison and Linda Gilden (New Hope Publishers, 2014) ISBN-10: 1-59669-398-3, ISBN-13: 978-1-59669-398-2

Unleash the Writer Within by Cec Murphey (OakTara Publishers, 2011) ISBN-13: 978-1-60290-307-4

Writers Market 2018 by Robert Lee Brewer (Writer's Digest Books; 97 edition 2017) ISBN-13: 978-1440352638, ISBN-1440352631

Christian Writers Market Guide 2017 by Steve Laube (The Christian Writers Institute, 2017) ISBN-978-162-184-0800

Formatting & Submitting your Manuscript - 3rd Edition by Chuck Sambuchino and the Editors of Writer's Digest Books (Writer's Digest Books, 2009) ISBN-13: 978-1-58297-571-9,
ISBN-10: 1-58297-571-X

An Introduction to Christian Writing - Second Edition by Ethel Herr (Highland Books, 1999) ISBN-1-892525-16-X

Fearless Writing by William Kenower (Writer's Digest Books, 2017) ISBN-13: 978-1-4403-4983-6, ISBN-10: 1-4403-4983-5

Pennies for your Thoughts by Holly G. Miller (Warner Press, Inc., 1990) ISBN 0-87162-501-6

On Writing Well – Fourth Edition by William Zinsser (Harper Perennial, 1990) ISBN 0-06-096831-1

The Writing World Defined A to Z by Sally E. Stuart, (Bold Vision Books, 2014) ISBN: 9780692360965

Sell & Resell Your Magazine Articles by Gordon Burgett, (Writers Digest Books, 1997) ISBN: 0-89879-799-3

Handbook of Magazine Article Writing by Michelle Ruberg, (Writers Digest Books, 2005), ISBN: 1-58297-333-4

Writer to Writer by Brodie and Brock Thoene (Bethany House Publishers, 1990) ISBN: 1-55661-042-4

Websites

Thewriteconversation.com

Janefriendman.com

Right-writing.com

Writersdigest.com

Almostanauthor.com

https://stevelaube.com/blog/

About the Author

Linda Gilden is an experienced, award-winning writer, speaker, editor, and writing coach. Author of the popular Love Notes series, she is also the author of *Mommy Pick-Me-Ups, Mama Was the Queen of Christmas, Personality Perspectives, Called to Write, Why You Do What You Do, Words to Live By, Called to Speak,* and several ghostwritten books. The *Linked Personality Quick Guides,* coauthored with Linda Goldfarb, will release soon. With over a thousand magazine articles to her credit, Linda Gilden loves to share a great story. As a freelance editor and writing coach, she encourages others to make their writing the best. As a member of the CLASSEMINARS training staff, Linda enjoys helping others polish their speaking and writing skills on their journeys to concise communication.

Linda Gilden's experience includes:

- Certified CLASS Seminar Trainer and Staff Member
- Director of CLASS Christian Writers Conference
- Director of Carolina Christian Writers Conference
- Board Member, CLASS Seminars, Inc.
- Certified Personality Trainer
- Cofounder of the Linked Personality System
- Former editor of *The Encourager,* print/web magazine of First Baptist Spartanburg, SC

- Frequent instructor at national writers conferences such as Glorieta Christian Writers Conference, Blue Ridge Mountains Christian Writers Conference, Florida Christian Writers Conference, Florida Writers Association Conference, Asheville Christian Writers Conference, Montrose Christian Writers Conference

- Developer and Coordinator of Get Published Now!™ program for new writers

- Freelance editor for publishing houses and numerous individual clients

- Graduate of the Institute of Children's Literature

- Judge for many Writer's Digest writing competitions

- Judge for many Christy Awards

- Teaches "Writing to Expand Your Ministry" in the Women's Ministry Program, New Orleans Baptist Theological Seminary

- Writing Team member for Presidentialprayerteam.com

- Columnist for Just18summers.com

- Columnist for thewriteconversation.com

- Columnist for Fox News' toddstarnes.com

- Member of **A**dvanced **W**riters and **S**peakers **A**ssociation, **A**merican **S**ociety of **J**ournalists and **A**uthors, **A**merican **A**ssociation of **C**hristian **C**ounselors, and **C**hristian **A**uthors **N**etwork.

Linda Gilden is a wife, mother, and grandmother. She finds great joy in time spent with her family. Her favorite activity is floating in a pool with a good book surrounded by splashing children! To find out more about Linda, her writing, and her ministry, visit www.lindagilden.com.